THE MOULDING OF A LIFE

by

Wendy Clark

Grosvenor House
Publishing Limited

All rights reserved
Copyright © Wendy Clark, 2013

Wendy Clark is hereby identified as author of this
work in accordance with Section 77 of the Copyright, Designs
and Patents Act 1988

The book cover picture is copyright to Wendy Clark

This book is published by
Grosvenor House Publishing Ltd
28-30 High Street, Guildford, Surrey, GU1 3EL.
www.grosvenorhousepublishing.co.uk

This book is sold subject to the conditions that it shall not, by way of
trade or otherwise, be lent, resold, hired out or otherwise circulated
without the author's or publisher's prior consent in any form of binding or
cover other than that in which it is published and
without a similar condition including this condition being imposed
on the subsequent purchaser.

A CIP record for this book
is available from the British Library

ISBN 978-1-78148-605-4

DEDICATION

I would like to dedicate this book to the memory of my daughter Nicola, and my parents who guided me through my early days, and still do even after their deaths in 2003 and 2010 respectfully.

Thanks to Mel who has supplied all the exotic butterfly photographs for the book cover.

Much gratitude to everyone who has encouraged me to finish this book, especially John and Dot. Many thanks to Melanie my eldest daughter, who has worked so hard typing all my notes. Also Clare and Rhiannon my other daughters, and grandchildren, Chloe, Kalum, Jacob, Nancy, and Grace who have all played an enormous part in the moulding of my life. But also my gratitude lies with the Spirit World who have inspired me with so much philosophy, and guided me on my spiritual pathway.

INTRODUCTION

It seems like only yesterday since I first became aware of the World of Spirit. In fact it was about forty years ago when my life had hit the depths of despair. My two year old little girl had passed away suddenly leaving a huge gap in my life. Through the blackness, feelings of pain surfaced suddenly throwing me back into the void which now had become my everyday world. The raw emotions that followed became a way of life for what seemed like eternity. This terrible event caused me in my turmoil to question what sort of God would allow a little child to die. My faith was in tatters, and it was only in this awful situation that my real journey began.

It is hard to decipher why life is taken for granted, it seems that living in the present time and appreciating what we have is so important, instead of longing for something more, which is hard to achieve. Losing anyone that we love is devastating, leaving us insecure and vulnerable.

During all bereavements we have guilt and regrets for things that we have done or not done. It is only when we begin to accept what has happened that we begin to bring peace to ourselves, and relinquish that hold we have on our loved one, and by doing that it is possible to let go of grief.

Eventually, we begin to survive life. It is a very slow process and there are no short cuts. It is necessary to experience the pain of grief in order to heal. Trying to return to some form of normality at a later date is not a betrayal of a loved one even though it may seem that way.

Chapter 1

EARLY DAYS

I suppose I led what I think of now as a pretty ordinary childhood, with working class parents, who like most, had to struggle to make ends meet. We lived in the West Midlands in a comfortable, but ordinary, terraced house with my grandparents, who doted upon me. My parents Joan and Ron were both in the Air Force and that was where they met. Dad was a Londoner and mum was from the outskirts of Birmingham. They were a perfect match. After they were married my father was posted to Gibraltar, so my mother did the natural thing in those days and lived with her parents in West Bromwich.

After the war, my father returned home, stating that he had won the war single handed. Everyone laughed, in good part, he was only a clerk, you see. In the late summer of 1948, I was born, but unfortunately, I was not what they hoped for. My name was supposed to be "Keith" and everything which had been purchased for my arrival was blue including my hair brush, which I still have in my possession today. As a child and from my own memories of childhood I was spoilt. The only child for five years of a loving couple, and also the apple of my grandparent's eye. But my world of security began to change in the year of 1953 when my mother was seriously ill after giving birth to my sister, in a home confinement. I'll never forget that chilly October morning. All night there had been a lot of commotion, and being small, I vaguely sensed that all was not well. So, bright and early that morning I was not really surprised when my father came into the bedroom to get me up, his eyes bright with excitement. As little as I was, I have never forgotten the words that he spoke to me, after he delivered the news that I had been sent a Christmas present early, and that it was a baby sister. He told me that it would not make any difference to the way he and mum loved me, for we were both as important to them. After the initial shock I became quite excited wanting eagerly to see the latest protégé, and I ran into the bedroom to see mum and my new sister. The little bundle by the side of the bed fascinated me so I approached it with some caution after being warned not to make a noise.

From that day my life changed, in what way, I am not quite sure, I assume as with most families, rejection and jealously set in. Looking back, after my sister was born mum was always ill and I suppose I felt neglected, but in actual fact this was only my imagination. As the days went by and the Doctor's visits became more frequent it was obvious even to me that mum was very ill. Eventually she was admitted to a sanatorium and my sister into a different isolation hospital. We all had X-rays taken and special injections. Dad's eyes were continuously red, and all I knew was that I was so sad to see my father crying, and I could not comfort him. He was never at home, for when he left work, he went to visit my mother and then my sister. If the time on the hands of the clock showed half past five and my father had not returned home,

THE MOULDING OF A LIFE

I became hysterical. Until one day the clock had to be turned round to face the wall so that I could not see it. This was the beginning of a vast life change which presented itself as total insecurity, which has always been part of my life as is obvious in the following pages. My mother had pulmonary tuberculosis and was in a sanatorium for eighteen months. My sister had meningitis caused by tuberculosis and was being cared for in a hospital a couple of miles away from my mother. In all that time I had no contact with either of them, for visiting was strictly forbidden, only my father was allowed to see them.

My world had shattered, the loving caring family had in my eyes, the eyes of a child, fell apart. My grandparents were really good to me, but ruled with a rod of iron at this time, which is probably what was needed. Later, as my mother improved she returned home, and I called her "Aunty" simply because I did not know who she was. I remember her now as if it were yesterday sobbing on my father's shoulder uncontrollably, when she knew that I had not recognised her.

Later on my sister also recovered, but now there was an even stronger bond between my mother and sister because of the near death experience the illness had brought with it. I felt a complete outsider.

The first painful memories of insecurity began when I used to get out of bed at night to check my parents were downstairs. I vividly remember, creeping along to the landing and listening to see if I could hear their voices above the television set, reassured, I would go back to bed and sleep.

I understand now why I did this, but at this time it was just a habit which had taken over my life and I was continually being scolded for it. My mother was so fed up with my getting in and out of bed that she used to tell me that a bell would ring downstairs every time I did it, but sadly this did not deter me, and I suffered many a telling off because of it.

Another recollection of how this insecurity manifested itself at that time was in little things such as our daily shopping excursions. As was my mother's way, we walked to town every day, and as times were hard she would walk the length of the town just to save a few pennies. It was post war years and many food items were still rationed. So inevitably, she would end up in Woolworth's and I was told to wait outside with my little sister, who was in her pram. I would watch my mother like a hawk as she weaved her way in and out of the counters to buy what was needed. There was no self-service in those days, all counters had assistants willing to serve customers, and there was mum hunting for bargains to make the house keeping money last the week. As soon as she disappeared from sight, I would dissolve into tears convinced she had abandoned me again, and inevitably got told off again. Please do not get me wrong I had a happy and contented childhood in many ways, but, as it is so with many parents they regard things as naughtiness at face value, without realising that they are symptoms of something deeper. I am very much to blame with my children and I think if most parents are honest, then they are too. For children are free spirits, entrusted to us, and it is our duty to be their guardians we do not own them We have the responsibility to bring them up to lead a full, and happy life, making them feel secure in the knowledge that we will always be there to love and guide them. We should not stifle them or give into their every need, so that they are completely reliant on us, and cannot stand on their own two feet in life. Life's lessons are hard, as I know personally, I do not wish my children to have to grow up and face the things which I have gone through.

All through my younger years I idolised my dad and repeatedly told him that I would marry him or someone like him when I grew up. To which he replied "They broke the mould when they made me."

Most of my school holidays were spent in London with my other grandparents. I loved their cockney accents and wanted desperately to be a cockney. The summers were endless and although I missed home I really enjoyed my holidays there.

When I was a little older, I remember my mother and father arguing, my dad would not stand up for my mum when she had a row with my grandparents. It resulted in my mum packing her case and leaving home. Dad and I with Susan in her pram trudged behind her to the bus stop, where she caught the bus and disappeared into the distance. Well, the wails and screaming that I managed at that event. I suppose it was insecurity rearing its ugly head again. We walked aimlessly along after the bus, dad trying to pacify us, but it didn't work. We carried on walking in the general direction that the bus had taken, for what seemed a life time. I expect it was an hour or so, my sister was crying and dad looked really upset. Suddenly there in the distance was mum walking towards us pretending that we were all invisible and trying to hide her embarrassment at her hasty actions. Dad was promptly ignored as he pleaded with her to come home, and I remember experiencing relief but anger at how she could put me through this hurt again. Well, eventually, all's well that ends well and mum returned home on the rash decision that dad should stand up to Grandma, and we would emigrate to Australia.

It was about the time when you could take this massive life changing experience for only ten pounds each. Drastic measures, you may think, but I hasten to add that it never came about, and in fact the only place we emigrated to was the front room. A wedge was driven between us and my grandparents. We ate in the front room and lived in there. At first it was like being on holiday, because the front room in those days was sacred, only used for high days, holidays and to entertain guests. Well the days went on and eventually it got to be a bit of a drag, carrying food and crockery from the kitchen through the middle room where my grandparents were, to the room we now lived in. I do not remember the way in which things were reconciled, but they were, and we drifted back into the usual routine of Grandma doing all the cooking, and us all eating together.

As I grew up, I subconsciously pushed the fears of insecurity to the back of my mind that is until I reached the end of my years at junior school. I still sucked my thumb and it was gradually wearing to a point, it became septic and was very painful, so I made a mental note to stop it. The habit was too hard to break and subsequently my teeth stuck out, and children can be very hurtful. I was termed "Goofy" or words to that effect. At the age of eleven or thereabouts children are very self-conscious and subsequently my self image was one of despair. I suffered chicken pox, and as a result sat the eleven plus examination alone in the Education Offices in our area. Much to my amazement, and that of my parents, I passed with flying colours, and won a place at

Grammar School. I did not want to go, as it meant leaving my best friend who had not been quite so lucky, and she was going to a Secondary Modern School. So here started another chapter in my life. A life to be dogged by insecurities which had stemmed from one main cause, but due to no one's real fault, yet everyone played a part. The moulding of a life is the responsibility of all who come into contact with that individual.

Chapter 2

GROWING UP

I looked forward to my first day at Grammar school with a little apprehension. Mum and dad had spent many hours collecting all the items of clothing and sports equipment needed for my days ahead.

I reported for school on my first morning, a little over-awed by the vastness of the building. Masters and Mistresses swept past in all their glory, dressed in black gowns and mortar boards in a wave of authority. I remember thinking how they resembled huge black crows, waiting to pounce upon their prey, namely us. After a brief tour of our new place of learning, we were sectioned off into various classes. I was assigned to a class of pupils all of average intelligence, while a friend of mine was allocated to an "express" form usually for children with prospects of a university education. Little did they know then that I was going to achieve my degree later in life? It was a tradition at the Grammar school that all first year students were targets and suffered the indignity of having their berets removed and the protruding tag pulled off the top. I remembered my mother's warning to take care of my beret with my life. Unfortunately, I attracted too much attention by doing this and my beret was uncoremoniously ripped from my hands. When it was thrown back at me there was a large gaping hole in the middle. Needless to say, I was not popular when I returned home that evening.

My time spent at Grammar school, was one of resignation more than enjoyment, I think looking back on it. Unless you happened to be a budding genius which I was not, you did not seem to warrant much attention.

My health up until the age of twelve had always been good, apart from the usual childhood illnesses which everyone suffers.

I think I was about thirteen years of age when a bit of bad luck befell me. It was a summer's day and mum was washing up in the kitchen, I was helping by drying the crockery. I remember commenting about a girl in school who was very good at doing "The Twist" which was extremely popular at that time. So, still clutching the tea towel I proceeded to demonstrate how the girl did the various moves. Suddenly my left knee dislocated, and I fell to the floor screaming in pain. Mum gazed on with a smile on her face and blankly asked, "Yes and then what did she do?" By this time with tears pouring down my face in pain, I did not know what to do, whether to laugh or cry because mum had obviously thought I was still copying the girl at school. She was panic stricken when she eventually realised what I had done and was nearly sick when she spotted my deformed knee. I was immediately whisked off to the local hospital and strapped up with strapping from my thigh to my toes. The weeks passed and my knee did not improve. It frequently dislocated when I was playing tennis, and got that bad that even when I was walking it would let me down and I found myself sprawled all over the pavement. It was most embarrassing. The noise of the bone returning to its normal place used to send shudders down my spine. Within a few weeks it was arranged for me to see an Orthopaedic Consultant at the District Hospital. As I had been working there on a voluntary basis for several weeks, to gain work experience, I was not really frightened.

The Consultant was very direct, and informed my parents that a large operation was necessary, which would leave a big scar, or maybe two. It involved a bone graft probably from my thigh, hence the two scars, and the tightening of tendons in my knee. Nowadays it would have been done by making a smaller incision, but not in the early sixties. The thought of being admitted to hospital did not appeal to me at all being a coward, but my parents said that I had no option.

It was also around this time that I had my front teeth extracted, as they had begun to stick out when my permanent teeth had come through. I could cope with that but I was not allowed to have any dentures for quite a long time, to enable my gums to settle. Children can be so cruel and I was constantly being ridiculed at school. So eventually I became resigned to the idea of admission to hospital, I suppose as a way of escape.

The day dawned, and with my case packed mum and dad duly delivered me to Salter Ward which was female surgical. Mum was upset and didn't want to leave me there. The ward comprised of women ranging from forty years of age to about eighty. I was not too impressed; it was really boring for a teenager. My bed was directly opposite a window overlooking the anaesthetic room leading into the operating suite and I was petrified.

The following day after my admission I was prepared for theatre. I dipped my thermometer into my early morning cup of tea; as I was not due to go to theatre until later in the day. I was found to have a high temperature and sent home much to my relief. Once I was safely installed at home I boasted about what I had done. Mum and dad were not very happy to say the least. About a month later, I was readmitted to another ward, which had a nicer atmosphere. It was comprised of beds for geriatric ladies, and also had a children's section. I often wish that I had the philosophy and teachings that I have now, mainly to live for one day at a time. I had really managed to get myself in such a state, right up to the morning of my operation. As there were no lift facilities to the ward, I was carried down the stairs on a stretcher cloth to an awaiting trolley. By this time I was very drowsy and thirsty after receiving my premedication an hour or so previously. I was given an injection and drifted off into insurmountable blackness. My first recollection of consciousness was one of pain and unceremoniously vomiting into a bowl which was being held for me by a nurse. I seemed to drift backwards and forwards into semi-consciousness for the next twenty four hours, until I surfaced completely. I was the proud owner of twenty two green sutures, and a multi coloured leg from thigh to toe. Thankfully the surgeon had managed to tighten the tendons in my knee, and transfer the bone within the joint without having to make an incision in my hip.

After a month, I was discharged from hospital complete with crutches, and under instructions to have physiotherapy, three times a week. Our front room became my bedroom, as I was unable to climb the stairs to bed. My parents were extremely supportive at this time, and arranged for my school work to be sent to me at home, worse luck! Every Monday, Wednesday and Friday I was taken by ambulance to the hospital for my exercises. I began to look forward to these little outings and as a special treat I was allowed to sit in the front of the ambulance with the driver. At physiotherapy I had heat treatment on my knee and then I had a contraption strapped to my ankle, with loads of weights added on each time I went for exercises.

After a few months the weights were so heavy that I was nearly dragged under the couch. Happily, though all's well that ends well, after nearly a year, I returned to school with only a slight limp. Adjusting back to school life was difficult, but not impossible. I had missed a trip to Switzerland which had caused some disappointment but obviously I was not meant to go.

There is one thing that I have become increasingly aware of, and that is that nothing happens by coincidence or chance, for I believe everything is personal responsibility, action and reaction, cause and effect, a balance in all things. Many times in our lives we see the effects of our actions, either by word or deed upon people with whom we come into contact every day. For we create our future days, in actual fact we are completely responsible for all that happens to us and we can blame no one but ourselves for own misfortunes, illnesses, pain and suffering and on the positive level our happiness, love and peace. If are happy and calm, we will radiate these things and other people will sense this and act accordingly to us. If on the other hand we send out into the atmosphere, panic and negativity then we will receive this back from people that we meet.

True happiness is very elusive to many people, but is a really very simple thing to achieve, it is a question of controlling one's thoughts, and pushing thoughts of worry away and living for the point of time, where you find yourself now. For, if we live in the past or the future, we are not truly living our lives to the full in the present moment.

This reminds me, back to the story. At this time in my adolescent years I had no idea that life had such deep philosophical undertones, and I was not conscious of the great Universal Law which controls all life.

I plodded on at Grammar school, never achieving much academically, until I was informed that I had to repeat a year's work, due to my absence from school. It was at this time I decided without a shadow of a doubt that my career lay in the nursing profession. Eventually, I was offered a placement at Bilston College of Further Education, as a pre-nursing student. My parents had difficultly at this time in obtaining permission for me to leave school, as it was an accepted rule in those days, that everyone stayed at Grammar School, until the age of sixteen, but, eventually permission was granted with a charge of ten pounds and I began my two year full time course.

College was so different, to the strict atmosphere of school life. Discipline was maintained but students were treated as adults, with more responsibility for their own education. I excelled in subjects such as Anatomy and Physiology and practical nursing, but I was sadly lacking in interest in subjects, such as Physics and English Literature. It was hard work, but we all enjoyed the course and attacked it with enthusiasm.

The practical side of nursing was always fun, especially as we had a male student who was always volunteered by the rest of us girls, to act as the guinea pig or involuntary patient. He did not appreciate it, especially when we held him down and attempted to pass a Ryle's tube into his nasal cavities and down into his stomach, but he took it in good part eventually, and became resigned to the role he had to play within the group.

One day, we had a First Aid examination. I had been chosen to be a patient with an open fracture of the lower arm. I was made up with artificial blood, and something that resembled a bone protruding through my arm. It was exceptionally realistic. As the lesson drew to a close, I completely forgot the make up on my arm, and shot off to catch the bus home. Well, I have never seen so many people turn a funny shade of green, everyone began leaping to their feet offering me a seat, in a very concerned manner, before I realised what I had done. It was not appreciated when I began to giggle at my mistake, and proceeded to peel the bone and extremely life like blood from my arm.

Whilst I was at college, mum had now returned back to work part time as a secretary. Grandma, now in her sixties had become increasingly thin, and did not look at all well. She was admitted to the hospital where I had worked on a voluntary basis, for tests. It was discovered that she had a cancerous growth in the lower part of her intestine, and also in one kidney. The surgeon decided to operate and perform a colostomy. Grandad, at this time was also ill. He suffered terribly with arthritic joints and heart trouble, so we were advised not to tell him of the seriousness of my grandmother's illness. The operation had been performed and all was satisfactory, but the following day, my grandmother had a relapse. The police were sent to the house, to fetch my mother who had just set out for work, my grandad was alone in the house, and was very upset to learn of what had happened in this way. A neighbour was dispatched to college, and took me back to the hospital. I stayed with my grandmother that night, as mum and dad had a difficult job in comforting my grandad.

I had at that time, no conception of life after death, but being at the side of my grandmother as she relinquished her hold upon her earthly life, was a great privilege and experience, that I will never forget. She regained consciousness a few times, and told me that there were several people standing by the vase of irises at the bottom of the bed, and she seemed very content and peaceful. As morning approached, and the dawn heralded another day, I felt my fears had been unfounded, and all would be well. I kissed my grandmother, not knowing that it was the last time that I would see her, and my father drove me home to bed whilst mum kept a vigil for the rest of the day. By tea time, it was over. My grandmother had passed away. Her life had not been in vain, for she had taught many things in her time to many people. Personally, she had taught me discipline, respect for all God's Creation, but most of all she had bought me love and security when I needed it most.

I had never experienced the loss of someone close before, I was only sixteen years old and it felt as if my whole world had collapsed. On the day of the funeral, I recall that the clock in her bedroom had stopped at the exact time that grandma had died. I remember grandad being unable to unlock the double wardrobe which he had shared with my grandmother, as he fumbled about in a daze, trying to get ready. The wardrobe had never done that before, so it was very strange. I was very aware of my grandmother's presence that day and it frightened me a little. Why it should I do not know, for she had never frightened me when she was alive, but the whole conception of the death and loss of someone I loved was totally new to me. I recall feeling very inadequate as I tried to console my grandad as he sat staring into the sky, huge tears rolling down his face. I realise now, after my own experiences that grief is a necessary form of expression, in order that we may come to an acceptance of change within our lives. It is an outpouring of emotion needed before we can come to terms with that loss. Inevitably, and it seems callous, but very true, people tend to cry for themselves, for they cannot see how they will be able to face life without their loved one, and the boundaries of life seem very hard at this time to cross. Now, I realise that love knows no bounds, and persons united in love are never separated.

Life carried on and we all went through various degrees of adjustment and growth at this time, some within the family more than others. Mum nearly had a nervous breakdown, and lost her voice as a symptom of grief. She had been sheltered up to that point, because all responsibility for the running of the household had been placed on my grandmother's shoulders at her own insistence. Therefore, mum had not been able to take the proverbial reins, as it were. Dad played a big part in consoling us all, and caring for grandad, whom he treated as his own father, with much love and respect.

I completed my course at college, and attained the necessary subjects needed to become a nurse. I attended for an interview at a hospital in Birmingham and was accepted to begin my student nurse training for State

Registration, in six months from that date. I was offered the post of cadet nurse until my eighteenth birthday.

So, now I began to achieve my aim in life at this time. I had my feet firmly planted, on the bottom rung of the ladder. I had now taken responsibility for my own life, or had I?

Chapter 3

THE FOUNDATION

I swelled with pride as I gazed in the mirror to be confronted with the new me. Here I was dressed in a smart crisp uniform, a nurse at last! Little did I know how much lay before me, before I could even consider earning the title of "nurse"? We met in the nurse's lounge, each laughing at the other in a dress that was unfamiliar to us all. From then on a type of comradeship was formed as we all embarked upon our new career together. Some fell quickly by the wayside, while others stayed the course and went on to achieve greater and better things.

I was now a cadet nurse, and along with all the other fledglings held my breath as we were allocated to our various wards and departments. To my disappointment, I was sent to the Pathological Laboratory, (Path Lab for short), to be assigned to the Haematology Department. That sounded impressive, I had not got a clue what it meant, except that it was something to do with blood. It was the study of blood, and the discovering of the biological changes within it during illness. Apparently the "Path Lab" had never had a cadet nurse, and were not too happy about the role that a "would be nurse" would play in their department. I was asked to report to the "wash up" room. I did not like the sound of that, but never the less I obeyed. Imagine my horror, when I realised that I had to empty and wash numerous specimen bottles, filled with blood and excreta. The smell was, overwhelming to say the least. All day I battled on, vowing, that if this was nursing I wanted no part of it. But that was only one day in my life the rest of my nursing career was much different.

Eventually, the cleaner, who had been ill, on my first day, returned to work. I was so grateful I could have kissed her. Then, I was allowed to go on to bigger and better things, or so I thought. I was taught to do cell counts and haemoglobin readings, which all seemed very professional to me.

The day arrived when I was sent onto the wards to take blood samples. We went to the maternity unit, a technician called Roger and I. He was very shy and went all different shades of pink, varying to beetroot red when he realised that the majority of the women were breast feeding. That was nothing to the funny colours that I went, when I swallowed a blood sample which I was pipetting. I hastily excused myself from the patient, gurgling incoherently, and was violently sick after I left the ward desperately hoping that the patient had not got hepatitis or something equally as awful.

Many things happened to me in the "Path Lab", I watched post mortems, off the record, of course, as our Sister Tutor thought we had no business concerning ourselves with the patients once they had departed this life. I can see her point of view, but being naturally curious I wanted to know what was in the body first hand. The first post mortem which I attended was terrible. I think it was the smell and the way in which the technician took it all in a day's work. Now, I have had more experience of life, and the proof of an afterlife, I realise that the body is but a vehicle in which the Spirit has form to learn upon the Earth Plane, and once the Spirit leaves and returns to the Spirit World the physical body is useless and becomes like a discarded overcoat. Since those early days, I have nursed many patients whose earthly lives have now ended, and I do not feel regret, but rather a privilege at being able to have touched their lives in some small way.

After three months, I was transferred to Ward B5, children's surgical. It was here, I learnt what discipline really meant. The ward Sister welcomed me, she was tiny, Welsh, and looked as if butter would not melt in her mouth. How young and inexperienced I was in those days! She made my time on her ward, hell! Even so, I learnt how to do things properly in the end. The lessons I learnt were never forgotten either, because even years later I half expected her to pop up behind me and start criticising.

She, who shall remain nameless, ruled the ward with a rod of iron. So many squares of the pattern on the counterpane each side of every bed, no talking amongst the nurses, no eating on the ward, and no slovenly or untidy attitudes, to recall but a few rules. The nurses feared her; the little patients loved her, for behind that efficient, starchy exterior she had a heart of gold and really cared about the children in her care.

My training got off to a flying start, and I mean that literally, the little ward Sister had a steadily growing dislike for me. I think that it all stemmed from the day when I dared to call one of the young dishy doctors by his Christian name. My mother and his mum were friends, so it obviously seemed the right thing to do. Unfortunately, Sister did not see it in quite the same light, and I spent a day scrubbing and polishing bedpans in the sluice as my penance. Some days later, I was on duty with Sister, when a Consultant, whom she really liked, strode up the ward to greet her. She flew towards him, and in her haste, slipped on the newly polished floor and skidded the last few feet towards him, sprawled on her back with her legs stuck up in the air. Unluckily for me I burst out laughing, after shaking uncontrollably for several seconds. She galloped to her feet, her face as black as thunder, eyes bulging, not a word did she utter. She raised her finger and pointed, strangely enough I knew exactly where I was meant to go. For the next few weeks I almost lived in the sluice, polishing bedpans so you could see your face in them. Apart from these minor setbacks, Ward B5 always had happy memories for me, because I loved working with children.

As I slowly went through my training, I felt in awe that people of all ages and backgrounds could be struck by terminal illnesses, and responsibility for their care was partially mine, I seemed to mature greatly, in order to fulfil the role I now played.

Night duty seemed a very glamorous and exciting prospect until the duty rota appeared on the notice board. I was allocated to Ward C3, Female Geriatric. Now, for some reason I enjoyed working with, and nursing male patients, more than female, I always found women more demanding, and idle than men when they were ill.

Our duty shifts started at eight o'clock in the evening and finished at eight o'clock the next morning. All day before my first shift, I had decided how tired I would be, working all night, so by the time that I went on duty I was absolutely worn out! Well, I reported for duty, to be greeted by Ward Sister slightly harassed by the worries of the day, and also the fact, that there was no Night Nurse to take charge that evening.

So, there I was, just my luck I thought, me, totally inexperienced as to the routine on nights, a ward full of old ladies, and an auxiliary nurse who seemed intent on knitting for the duration of the shift. She gazed at me with distaste as Sister gave the report and said she hoped that everything would be alright, (no more than I did). She also said that there was always a Night Nursing Officer to call on, if I needed help. Then, she casually informed me that three patients were seriously ill and would probably die in the night and with that rather worrying comment, she disappeared with a wave of her hand, down the corridor, and home to bed. I was alone, or so I felt, with the responsibility of thirty two lives dependant on me. What an ego! How much I had to learn, but during that never ending night that was exactly how I felt.

Wherever I went into the ward, I was followed by the constant click of knitting needles I think that the auxiliary nurse had them glued to her arms, and her sole occupation in life was to manufacture large, baggy jumpers. Her work was conspicuous by its absence. Compassion and caring were words that did not enter her vocabulary, and I think her life would have been more fulfilling in a different role.

During the long night that followed and seemed to last for eternity, three patients died, as had been predicted by Sister. They went one after another, until

I was convinced that there was a conspiracy against me. But, joking apart I still felt very privileged to be a part of someone's transition to the World of Spirit.

Whatever anyone says about death, it is but an instant of time through which we travel, and there should be no fear, but a loving acceptance of what is, and a relinquishing of our lives to God. For I feel that until people can come to a stage of accepting death, which is a very taboo subject, they cannot live their lives fully, because, surely dying is a part of living.

So, to return to my first spell of night duty, after the Doctor had certified the patient's deaths, my last duty to them was to lay them out before they were taken to the mortuary.

As the sun rose on a new day, and the shift drew to a close, I felt that I had gained a little more insight into the overall cycle of life, and as I crawled into bed exhausted, I fell into a deep sleep.

Chapter 4

A LESSON TO LEARN

Three months of night duty ended, and I eagerly scanned the new allocations list, to see what my future ward would be. Great, Ward C5, Men's Surgical. Surgical nursing had always held a special interest for me, although I sometimes felt cheated, missing out on one of the most important parts of the patient's treatment, the operation, and I think I mentioned before that I much preferred nursing male patients

Jenny, my friend had been sent to C3, the ward on which I had worked on night duty, I did not envy her, the ladies were very nice, but it was a very depressing ward, as not many of the patients improved to the extent of being discharged into the community. Secretly I was quite pleased with my lot.

I reported to the ward to be greeted by a pleasant ward Sister. She was, I was about to learn, a very good teacher and a compassionate nurse, and although I held her a little in awe, we seemed to get off to a good start. Little did I know that it was to be here that I made one of the biggest mistakes of my life, and I would spend the next ten years paying for it?

THE MOULDING OF A LIFE

The ward comprised of thirty six beds, containing the same number of male patients, of varying age. Some were nearing the end of their lives, while others had hardly begun. All in all, they were not a bad bunch, although they liked a laugh and a joke with the nurses, the majority would help with the different duties to pass the time.

A young nurse came to the ward and became highly popular with Sister, after washing thirty six thermometers (which, incidentally, were like gold) under the hot water tap, exploding them all. I did not live that down for a long while.

The men were a lot of fun, although, one afternoon I was not impressed with the antics of several of them. It had been a hectic morning, ward rounds, dressings, bed baths, and so on, I was now trying to complete the two o'clock observation round about half an hour late. As I approached Bill's bed he was snoring his head off, so I decided to take his pulse without waking him. He was quite a large hefty man, and a chronic asthmatic, he looked very angelic as he lay there breathing perfectly normally, for once. Gently, I lifted his hand out from under the counterpane, trying not to disturb this peaceful sleep which he seemed to be enjoying. Unsuspectingly, I looked down as I was busily counting his pulse, only be confronted by a hairy ape type hand with large claws on it. I screamed, much to the delight of the other patients, who had plotted this dastardly deed, and I fled up the ward trying desperately to regain, my now shattered image of cool composure. I survived, and was constantly reminded of how the "lads" had got their own back on me for all the injections and treatments, they had suffered under my hands, but it was taken in good part.

It was after I had got used to the routine of the ward that we had a young man admitted by the name of "Robert" or "Bob", as he liked to be known. Something about the easy way he spoke attracted me to him, and still being quite young and impressionable, I am afraid that I broke one of the golden rules of nursing. I got involved emotionally with a patient. Maybe it was the uniform; he was at that time a soldier in the Army, stationed in a little place called Watchet in Somerset.

The following day Bob went to the theatre and had a very inflamed appendix removed, which was just about to perforate.

Surprisingly enough he had no pain, but had eaten half a bar of soap to induce stomach ache to get extra leave from camp. I should have realised then, how easy it was to be deceived by him, but they say that love is blind. After he was discharged we kept in touch and then we went out with each other as often as our shifts allowed.

During this time I had left the ward and returned to Study Block, in the School of Nursing. We worked hard, but we also liked to have a good laugh. Our Sister Tutor, who took the class for anatomy and physiology, was exceptionally strict and aptly enough bore the proud name of Sister Stern. Just before her lecture was due to start, a couple of other nurses and myself, decided to rearrange Charlie slightly. Charlie was our human skeleton, who gazed at us, whilst hanging from a stand at the front of the lecture room. We set about our dastardly deed, giggling and wondering what reaction we would get from our tutor. We stood back to admire our handiwork. Charlie was suspended in mid-air in a most undignified way. We had folded his bony arms and legs in such a way that he resembled a very emaciated Russian dancer. His jaws, attached to his skull by a strong spring, were clamped in a fierce grimace, a pencil tightly clasped between his teeth. He looked as if he was enjoying a long awaited cigarette. Hastily we resumed our seats, trying to appear as angelic and innocent as possible. In she strode with a frightening air of authority; we quivered in anticipation, waiting for the explosion. Nothing! Not even a flicker of recognition of our labours showed in her severe features. Sadly, we were disappointed. How could she fail to notice our masterpiece? Secretly, I felt quite relieved; maybe we had gone a bit overboard this time. The lecture progressed; it was all about the functions of the blood. Each time Sister turned her back to write on the board, we threw looks of concern to each other. Five minutes to go before the lecture ended, Charlie was still swinging there, fiendishly smoking and dancing still totally invisible, or so it seemed to Sister Stern. Then suddenly with no warning, she pounced. In a shrill, uncontrolled screech she demanded to know who had the audacity to do such a terrible thing to a valuable piece of hospital equipment. We trembled in terror. Was this really our very self-controlled tutor of just a few moments before?

I wished that the floor would just open up and swallow me or better still just her. We were all too petrified to own up to our daring crime, so she strode backwards and forwards in front of us, looking deep into our eyes, until we were sure she could read our minds and detect who were the guilty culprits.

Charlie, still perilously swinging at the front of the classroom, decided to do a death defying pirouette as she charged passed him catching his bony elbow with her starched uniform. Her eyes dull and expressionless and her face were as black as thunder. All at once I had an uncontrollable urge to burst out laughing; I bit my lip instead and nearly choked. Looking back I think it was partly due to hysteria, partly fright. All I knew was that I wanted to be a million miles away from this classroom. Eventually, under so much pressure and the threat of all off duty being cancelled, we had to own up; we slowly walked dejectedly, to the front of the classroom, our eyes firmly fixed to the floor. There we suffered the full wroth of our Sister Tutor's anger, who continued to expound the fact that good nurses were expected to behave responsibly. It all sounded a bit boring to me, if you couldn't have a bit of a laugh occasionally. It was as if she read my mind, instantly she commanded me to restore Charlie to his former glory. Eager to please I unravelled his long bony legs so that they once again dangled precariously towards the floor. Then I quickly yanked the pencil from between his rigidly clamped jaws. Oh, dear, unfortunately poor Charlie's teeth were not as stable as I had first thought, for, as he finally relinquished his grip on the pencil, his molars, premolars and incisors flew in different directions, like guided missiles to every corner of the room. I looked on in horror, not knowing whether to laugh or cry. Sister Stern whose calm, serene and expressionless face was now distorted and unrecognisable, to say the least, dismissed the rest of the class who rushed from the lecture room whispering and taking bets as to what my fate would be. I shivered in my shoes as I envisaged the possibility of being completely dismissed from nurse training.

She who must be obeyed, rummaged through a desk drawer, and with a dry grin brandished a tube of glue, and without one word pointed to the toothless fiend dangling like something from a horror movie a few feet away from me. Then, with one almighty flourish the Tutor swept from the room.

I gazed at Charlie thoughtfully, I wondered if the proud owner of this skeleton was looking down on me at that moment in anger, or was he laughing at my predicament. Quickly I scoured the floor for teeth, and began with some difficulty, I might add, to reconstruct his upper and lower jaws. I never was any good at jigsaw puzzles, and as I stood back to admire my handiwork the effect was even more horrific. Looking back I think now that it took me at least three hours to restore him to something like his former glory. I missed my date that night, and my supper, and I've hated him ever since.

My off duty time was not spent studying as it should have been, since I had started dating Bob. We had, in a short time become very serious about each other, and in a space of a few months were foolishly talking about marriage. Looking back it seemed the right thing to do, but now I can see that an overwhelming commitment such as marriage is not something that you rush into after several weeks without knowing what you are letting yourself in for. This was to be almost one of the biggest mistakes of my life, and the more my parents dissuaded me, the more I was determined to make it. Whose life was it anyway?

Foolishly I left my training, and turned my back on this life of glamour, of black stockings and dishy doctors, which in reality revolved around bed pans, suffering and pain. Just like a fairy tale, I had been swept of my feet by a handsome soldier, whom I had tended whilst he was sick. How naive and immature I was, soon my happiness was to burst like a bubble, so real and yet so fragile.

In the meantime I had found that I was pregnant, I was horrified, and in those days it was certain disgrace and humiliation. Eventually I broke the news to my parents, they were really upset, and their dislike of my future husband became more and more intense. Frequently they pleaded with me not to marry, but instead to have the baby adopted, and they would stand by me. Isn't it strange, looking back they were right, but you know how teenagers are, if they are told to do one thing, they tend to do exactly the opposite, and I was no means an exception to the rule?

We had a small, unimpressive wedding in a registry office in Smethwick, and within five minutes it was all over. No reception, nothing. I really had upset my parents. They excused themselves and went home, mum in tears, and dad looking very upset. Now that I am a parent I can appreciate the feelings that they must have been experiencing at this time, but I was so elated at the time that did not matter and very selfishly, I ignored how they felt, convincing myself that they would get over it in a few weeks.

It started soon after, the arguments, the string of frequent affairs with various girls where he was stationed. How stupid I had been. Who was he? I hardly knew this person with whom I had entrusted my life. Ironically three days after the wedding I had a miscarriage, and for a long time thought that it was a punishment for my misdeeds.

The posting to Berlin which we were going on, did not materialise, and his visits home on weekend passes became less and less frequent. There was always some excuse as to why I should not move to Somerset where he was stationed. I began working as a dental nurse in a large teaching hospital in the centre of Birmingham.

Loneliness is a terrible thing, and here I was barely nineteen, living in the role of a married woman, already I had given up my career in general nursing, and I must admit I felt quite let down. The mind is a wonderful thing, for as we think so we become. I repeatedly convinced myself that this situation was alright, it was just an unfortunate phase in my life, everything would soon sort itself out, just like in the books, and I would live happily ever after. Looking back perhaps I had not been allowed to grieve for my unborn child, so tiny - and yet when I had seen it, so perfect in every detail. A small carbon copy, of a real person.

In this day and age, it is a recognisable fact that the survivor of a miscarriage does not receive the support and sympathy from others, as in the loss for instance, of a child who has established it's "place" in society. Sometimes death by miscarriage or of a new-born baby may be virtually ignored.

Friends and relatives can also assume that this death can be righted by the birth of another child, and generally fail to understand the deepness of the loss experienced by the survivor.

I left my job as a dental nurse and set off one weekend to look for accommodation in a little harbour village called Watchet in Somerset, two miles away from the Army barracks where my husband was stationed. Luckily I found a house to rent, overlooking the sea, it was spacious, had a large garden, and it gave me the feeling that I was on holiday all the time. My husband muttered his approval, although I think it cramped his style to have me hanging around him, but I set about making the best of a bad job, and tried to knuckle down to being a proper wife.

We lived in Watchet for about two years where I worked in a geriatric hospital until my husband was medically discharged and then we returned home to live on the outskirts of Birmingham. It was a far cry from the country life that we had been used to, all things seemed geared to a much faster pace of life in the town, and it was really hard to adapt.

Soon, after our return, I gave birth to our first little girl, Nicola, she had blonde hair and blue eyes, and we were both so proud, I think it was at that time in our marriage we became very close, and now, I thought perhaps, the fairy tale would come true.

A few years later, still unable to settle in a town, Bob and I took Nicola and moved to North Wales. We were very lucky, both finding work in a local hospital, Bob as a porter and myself as a nurse. In the day time Nicola, who was now two years of age, was cared for in a nursery nearby called "Kiddielands", where she had great fun. Again we had been very fortunate and managed to rent a bungalow near to the sea front, it was called "Que Sera" (what will be, will be!). I was not aware of the significance of this name until two weeks later, when Nicky was taken seriously ill. If only I had known what I know now, I would never have left her to go to work, for her life was to be very short, but in it she gave lots of joy and love to all that came into contact with her.

Chapter 5

NICOLA

The winter of 1971 came upon us, with a vengeance. It was almost Christmas and recently we had celebrated Nicola's second birthday. Power strikes had hit us badly as everything in our rented new home was controlled by electricity. It was February and the weather was really chilly so we were desperate for the power cuts to end.

I had been feeling unwell and so I decided to visit our local doctor. Much to my amazement, not only did he diagnose me as having mumps, he also found out that I was in the early stages of pregnancy.

That evening as Nicola splashed about in her bath, complete with ducks, boats and all manner of other things, I tried to explain to her that a baby was growing in my tummy. She was really excited and demanded that it come out now, so that she could play with it. She never saw that baby as she passed away a few months later.

Christmas came and went the power strikes increased in number. Luckily we had a coal fire so we managed to keep warm with a constant supply of logs.

It was a Friday afternoon when I collected Nicola from "Kiddieland', a nursery where she was cared for whilst I worked as a nurse in a nearby hospital. It was a relief that the weekend had arrived, perhaps I could catch up with some housework. I had tended to let things slide as I had been suffering with morning sickness, and some mornings it was all I could do to drag myself into work. At present I was working in the Outpatients Department, the hours suited me, only working from nine o'clock until three.

As I hurried to collect my daughter, one of the staff informed me that she had not been her usual self, probably due to the onset of a cold. At the time I did not pay too much attention to it, as there was always one virus or another doing the rounds. We went home and as I was preparing supper, my husband Bob called me, Nicola had vomited.

Next day apart from her cold she seemed to be fine, until evening time when she vomited again.

I telephoned the local surgery only to be informed that if I wanted her to see a doctor, I could bring her in. The receptionist said there was a twenty four hour virus doing the rounds at present. We decided to leave it until the next morning as the temperature outside was well below freezing point by that time. It did not seem a good idea to take her out into the cold night air.

Nicola slept soundly and crept into bed with us for an early morning cuddle, she was a very loving child. Suddenly she was violently sick, so we called the doctor, who promised to visit us within the hour. Nicola drifted off to sleep and I was unable to wake her. As a nurse you are trained to help anyone in an emergency, but as soon as the patient is someone you love and is totally dependent on you, sheer panic sets in. The doctor arrived, he was a very welcome sight, and as he gravely began to examine our little girl, she started to have a fit. Quickly he advised us not to bother with an ambulance but to take Nicola as fast as we could to the hospital where we were both employed.

The journey that Sunday afternoon seemed never ending, but it probably took under ten minutes. My main concern was to stop Nicola from choking as she had begun vomiting again and was only semi-conscious. As we rushed into Casualty we were greeted by the team who were awaiting our arrival. Nicola was given an injection of paraldehyde to control the convulsions as they were becoming really severe. She was then taken up to the wards whilst it was decided what tests were necessary. A lumbar puncture was carried out and while this took place we were advised to leave the hospital for a few hours. So under protest we did as we were told, still in a state of shock, but not fully grasping the seriousness of the situation.

Bob was of little support to me, he had vanished to chat to a nurse, with whom he was very friendly, in fact over friendly. I had my suspicions that they were having an affair but at that time I couldn't have cared less.

During the hours that followed no one seemed to know what was best for my daughter. The convulsions were almost under control now and she was unconscious. She looked so helpless lying there, slipping further and further away from me. I spent all night sitting at her bedside praying that God would make her better. It was terrible to see her so still and lifeless, but I was convinced that something could be done, but no one seemed to have any idea what was causing her condition. One of the nurses came to me and asked if it were possible that she may have drunken something poisonous, but I knew that was not likely as everything dangerous was kept well out of her reach.

After a long night of praying in the Chapel, and keeping vigil by Nicola's bed, the morning eventually dawned. It was a typical Monday, dull and damp, a heavy mist hung over the sea, giving it a slightly foreboding appearance. Was it really only a few days ago that I had been looking forward to a weekend off duty, and here I was in such unbelievable circumstances, with our little girl fighting for her life. Still no one was aware of what she was fighting, and no one even a step nearer to helping her medically.

A Specialist Consultant in Neurology was visiting from Liverpool to do his fortnightly clinic in Outpatients. I normally worked with him as his nurse, but today things were a little different, here I was begging him to examine my daughter, privately, if necessary. He was my last hope! He readily agreed and within minutes he had decided that emergency surgery was the only option. He advised burr holes into my little girl's head to release the pressure, which he had diagnosed, had been building up within her brain causing vomiting and also the violent fits. Preparations for this were undertaken straight away, this included shaving off all her blonde hair, and putting her onto a respirator, so that she was no longer breathing for herself. Although all of this seemed like a nightmare, there were times when I was sure that it was not really happening and I was playing a part in a play. Times when I felt totally detached from the situation, as if I was standing back, watching it happen to somebody else. I am sure many parents in the same sort of situation have felt exactly the same. I began to feel strangely calm, it was going to be alright at least they were doing something now, not just letting her die without a fight.

By three o'clock that afternoon my tiny, lifeless child was in theatre, by six o'clock she was returned to the ward, along with many monitors and technical equipment. As the surgeon approached me, I eagerly scanned his face for any glimmer of hope, he avoided my eyes as he told me that a brain biopsy had been done, and it had been discovered that Nicola's brain was so inflamed that if she survived she would be permanently brain damaged. He also added that the cause was due to the mumps virus! In those few minutes my world collapsed, I could not take it all in; somehow it did not seem possible that mumps could cause this. It was my fault I'd given it to her! Somewhere, as if in the distance, in a state of unreality, I heard the consultant saying that if her temperature dropped suddenly, it would be necessary to warm her up immediately, although this in itself would be enough to kill her, because it would aggravate the brain tissue and inflame it even more. Suddenly everything became hopeless. I sat by her bed, listening to the constant clicking of the respirator, holding her little hand in mine. Oh how I wished that we had not moved here, perhaps it would not have happened if we had stayed in Birmingham!

A Minister appeared at the side of the bed he tried to console me, and then gave Nicola the Last Rites. In my confused and bewildered state, God had not only let Nicola down, but also me. I had prayed and trusted in Him to help Nicola, and where was He now when we both so desperately needed Him?

I did not realise at that particular time that my daughter was a gift from God to me, and now it was time for Him to take that gift back. I would always be her mother whatever happened and would always have her near to me within my heart for no one can take away precious memories. Another thing that I did not comprehend at this time was that life is eternal this life is but just a small particle of the whole. We are not punished by God, but rather we are the victims of life.

That night the nursing staff became concerned about my condition, and was afraid that I may miscarry due to my distressed state. As I was sleeping in the hospital to be near my daughter, they insisted that I take some sleeping tablets, which I did under protest. About one o'clock in the morning, heavily sedated, I stumbled into the ward to be greeted by the incessant clicking of the respirator, which was at that time sustaining Nicola's life. She was being nursed on a one to one basis by a nurse, who was also a nun.

As I broke down by the bedside, she told me how it would be a happy release for my daughter, if God were to take her now. Feelings of anger overwhelmed me to such an extent that I wanted to hit out at her, knowing inwardly that she was speaking the truth. I left the ward and automatically headed for the sanctuary of the hospital Chapel. It was here that I stayed for the rest of that long night, still hoping for some miracle to happen.

Another morning dawned, cold and foggy. People went busily about their business in the hospital, just as I, myself usually did. My parents arrived from Birmingham with my sister Susan. Mum who had said that everything would be alright with all the modern technology that was available, collapsed into a heap when she and dad were ushered it the side ward, where their Grandaughter lay, wired up to all manner of equipment which was only just managing to sustain her. Only a couple of hours previously Nicola's body temperature had dropped rapidly, and so now, every effort to keep her warm was being employed.

I felt and surely looked a wreck by now, but unusually for me, I could not have cared less. Mum and dad insisted that I leave the hospital for an hour, to go home to wash and freshen myself up. Something deep inside me told me not to leave it was as if I was not there to will Nicola to live she would give up her fight for life, but my parents were very firm with me, promising that we would keep in touch with the hospital by telephone. Then reluctantly, and still under protest they led me away.

As soon as we arrived home and I saw Nicola's toys and clothes about the place, the harsh reality of it all hit me with a vengeance. We rang the hospital, only to be informed that there was no change in her condition. So when we returned an hour later, we were not prepared to find the screens around the bed, and no one seemed to be able to look us in the eye. In a few moments the doctor came to greet us, his eyes also avoided mine, he told me that Nicola had died a few minutes earlier, and that she had been very peaceful at the end.

I did not know what happened then, except to say that the floor seemed to come towards me at an alarming pace, and everything went black. As I fought my way back, through the darkness which enveloped me, I remember thinking they have made a mistake, they must mean someone else. But it was true, and when I had recovered sufficiently, I was taken to the bedside of my little girl. I'll never forget it; she lay there so still and so peaceful. I tried to pick her up, to hold her for one last time in my arms, but they stopped me. Someone had put a lily in her tiny hands, and a small knitted white hat covered her head hiding the baldness and the scars where the burr holes had been made the day before, when we had been so hopeful that something could be done to save her life.

I was taken home and sedated, frequent waves of grief overcame me, and my family were all numb with shock and the abruptness of the end. Where was the explanation, for what reason had all this happened? What was the point of bringing a life into the world for it to be extinguished, so easily and finally, for no apparent reason? Little did I know that Nicola would always be with me, but I did not realise this until many years later, when I was given a poem from Spirit, which helped me to have some closure on my loss. I hope that it will help other parents who have been in the same situation.

The sorrow of losing a loved one, especially one so young,
Will haunt you for all your waking hours but realise you have to be strong.
For think of the memories and love that you hold, to cherish and nurture as you would gold.
A life that was put into your care, so that part of it you should share.
Remember these words in your heart as you grieve and desperately try the past to retrieve
The soul of the loved one, who has left you now,
Is there by your side forever to care and guide you somehow.
Gain strength in the knowledge she lives in not this world but another.
And know in your heart you will always be her mother.

My parents took charge of the funeral arrangements and, although she had only died on Tuesday, the funeral was to be held in Colwyn Bay on Friday morning.

February the eleventh dawned. It was the day that I had been dreading since Nicky had died three days before. Drugged on phenobarbitone prescribed by my doctor to keep me calm, all was very surreal and dream-like.

The funeral was to take place at the nearest crematorium in Colwyn Bay. My parents had made the arrangements for the coffin of my little girl to be taken straight there, to avoid the distress of following the hearse.

It was a dull, cold and dreary day, my legs nearly buckled as I saw the little white coffin at the front of the small chapel. I had not been allowed to see Nicky since her death as my parents had thought it was better to remember her as she was a playful toddler full of life. Knowing what I do now I wish that I had seen Nicky and kissed her goodbye, but I realise that my parents were doing what they felt was best at the time.

The only part of the service I can remember is the singing of "The Lord is My Shepherd" and "All Things Bright and Beautiful"; the rest is a foggy dream. Everyone was crying as we left her behind in that little chapel on a day that will be etched in my memory forever.

The next few weeks were spent in a haze, in a feeling of wanting to talk about what had happened, over and over again, in a way it seemed to bring me closer to Nicola, but the pain it bought with it was a physical pain, one of utter despair and worst of all helplessness.

It is at this time, that any parent who has been bereaved will know, a feeling of failure continually pursues you. For a parent is there to protect and care for a child in whatever circumstances, and not to comply with this, is classed as failure. We look to our parents even as we become older, for advice and guidance always assuming that they know best and are aware of answers to questions that we ask, but this is not always the case and inside them too, lurks the small child which is inside us.

Guilt, failure, disbelief and confusion reigned. So many unanswered questions! It is when people are bereaved that they feel so unable to control the situation that they usually need to blame someone for what has happened. Many people blame the doctors, or sometimes the accusing finger is pointed to God. I was by no means an exception, and it was God who had the full force of my anger.

The days came and went, time merged into eternity. Visitors stopped by, but most felt it easier to send a card or flowers rather than to talk about Nicola's death. I learnt at this time how the majority of human beings are unable to cope with the grief of others. Perhaps they have to face up to their own immortality by acknowledging the grief displayed by another.

Clichés said hastily to bridge an unwelcome silence, such as "God never gives us anymore than we can cope with", echoed incessantly around my head until I could scream. Or, even "God only takes the best" said reassuringly to make me feel better, only made me want to shout "Take them WHERE?" Was I going crazy? Is there somewhere else? Who was undressing her and caring for her, and doing all the things that I did? Who was I? No longer a mother, I was no longer worthy of that title now.

I listened to children passing our window on their way to school, "Mummy" they shrieked, trying to attract their mother's attention, and all too quickly I would leap up ready to respond and then would sink dejectedly into a chair. During these dark months that followed Nicola's death my life had been put on hold. I welcomed sleep but hated waking up to face the stark reality of life without my little girl who had bought so much happiness.

Why do we take life for granted and not appreciate what we have in the present time? All too soon our chances of showing our feelings and affection are snatched away from us, and it's too late. How I longed for just a second chance, a few minutes to turn back the clock and make everything alright again. Something I find very hard to live with is that she had regained consciousness once, several hours after her admission. I had been sent away while a lumbar puncture was being performed, it was during this brief time Nicola had cried for "Mummy", and sadly I was not there. This is something I have to live with, which even now hurts.

During all bereavements we have guilt's and regrets for things done or not done. It is only as we begin to accept what has happened that we eventually bring peace to ourselves, and relinquish that hold which we have on our loved one, and by doing that we have let go of grief, knowing full well that it will never let us go. Eventually, we begin to survive life without the child or the person that we have lost. It is a very slow process but we cannot go around the circumference of grief, we have to go through the middle of it to survive as a whole person.

Letting go of grief is not a betrayal of a loved one, it is an acknowledgment that life continues even though it can never be the same. The bond of love between two people never dies, especially as I was to find out later, between mother and child.

Pain and suffering is the channel through which the learning of greater things can be achieved.

Chapter 6

A NEW BEGINNING

Strangely enough, I do not recollect very much of my pregnancy, except to say that I spent most of it clothed in black. My time was spent reading and re-reading the cards that were sent with the funeral flowers, somehow they bought me comfort realising that other people had shared in my grief. one of the cards sent from our neighbours bore the words "To our shining star Nicola", I took comfort in knowing that she was looking down on me from somewhere in the heavens. My mind was in turmoil, I was terrified that everyone would forget the existence of my little girl and I was determined to be a constant reminder to others. My biggest fear was that everyone close to me would be whisked away with no word of explanation and I would be helpless to stop it. This was my constant nightmare, and another example of insecurity rearing its ugly head in my life. Deep down it was as if everyone that I loved was taken from me. I became especially clingy towards my husband, frightened that he would be involved in an accident or some such incident. Perhaps the reader may think it odd that my husband was not mentioned much during previous pages, this was due to the fact that he was not very supportive, and did not show much concern for the terrible tragedy that had taken over our lives. Looking back, and now being a little more aware, I have begun to realise how complex human relationships can become. I think that we were both grieving in our individual ways and not communicating that grief to each other and sharing the burden that it bought with it. Possibly if we had allowed ourselves to become united in our sorrow, our marriage would have survived. I have recently discovered after carrying out some research into this subject that ninety percent of couples who lose a child, have marital problems within a year of the child's death. It is a testing time, and a marriage that was not strong before the death of a child, tends to become much weaker after that experience.

I carried on working at the hospital for a short time after Nicola's death. I had been given eight days compassionate leave, and it was generally agreed that I would be better occupied back at work than moping around the house all day alone. So I returned to the Out Patients Department, it was not the answer. Glances of pity only increased my need to talk of my sadness and everyone very cleverly bypassed the topic, if it were at all possible.

Time was telling on my size, I was growing rapidly, now being nearly four months pregnant, I had great difficulty in squeezing into my uniform.

July was an exceptionally hot month; I had left work in June, and was rushed into a local nursing home with a haemorrhage. The doctors were well aware how precious our new baby was to us and ordered complete bed rest for a few days. When I was feeling a little stronger, Bob and I decided to go into Rhyl for an evening meal. It was a little treat in an endeavour to cheer us both up.

In fact it was quite a big step for us both, as this was the first time that we had been out socially since the death of our daughter. It is very common in bereavement for the survivors to feel that to enjoy oneself is actually in some ways being a traitor to the memory of that person. That is why it was such a landmark, and that which we would have tackled normally, seemed to take so much effort in those first dark days.

The evening turned out to be very enjoyable, and for a short time we both took on a role of being a normal, carefree, young married couple out for an evening on the town. Unfortunately, it turned out be quite a memorable night as suddenly I found myself in labour, right in the middle of my dessert. Today was July the eighth, two months before my baby was due to put in an appearance. The first and foremost thought in everyone's mind was that I would never cope if this child did not survive I think it would have finished me off in fact. So without further ado, I was rushed twenty miles for a very bumpy ride in an ambulance to St Asaph Hospital.

A midwife came along for the journey, and frightened me to death by telling me that she had delivered a baby the night before on the same route. I decided that she was not going to have a repeat performance, and hung on to my little bundle as if it were possible to stop its imminent escape.

It seemed like hours before we arrived at our destination, a small cottage hospital in a little village which proudly owned a large Cathedral, thus making it one of the smallest cities in Wales.

H.M. Stanley Hospital was different from the majority of local hospitals mainly because it boasted the only Premature Baby Unit in the vicinity. This is the reason that I had been hastily transported to the relative safety of a hospital which owned the most important incubator. A must if my baby who was eight weeks early was to survive.

Hastily, I was transferred onto a convenient bed by my escort who wished me "All the best", and disappeared down a nearby corridor. A doctor appeared and reassuringly explained that I was in good hands, although at the time I was not paying much attention because I was violently vomiting as I had been for much of the twenty mile journey. All I wanted was for it to be over, so that I knew my baby was safe. Everything was a blur; just a feeling of unreality as the pethidine injection sent me into a false drowsy state.

As I drifted back into consciousness with each contraction, I was aware of a feeling of peace and acceptance around me. I think that Spirit was close to me even then. It was as if I had at last come to a realisation that whatever happened would be what was meant to be, and suddenly, I had no fear for what the coming hours would bring, it was all out of my control.

Melanie was delivered just before dawn on July 9th 1972, the tiniest baby I had ever seen, weighing in at three pounds and three ounces. In the delivery room nurses were alerted into action on her arrival. I caught a glimpse of her and then she was whisked from the room and placed into an incubator under the watchful eye of specialist paediatric staff. (I must add that although in this day and age it is the accepted norm for the survival of babies much smaller than Melanie, in 1972 medical science had not progressed to anywhere near the stage that it has in the modern day.)

A sense of relief and accomplishment swept over me as I thanked God for the safe delivery of my daughter, who had unceremoniously been swept away with a flurry of starched uniforms and a procession of electrical monitors.

I slipped into a deep sleep, exhausted still unable to grasp that it was all over, my mind first churning over the events of the preceding hours. Had I dreamt it all, I wondered?

Suddenly I came to my senses, panic flooding to the forefront of my mind. Where was my baby, perhaps she had died and they were frightened to tell me? I had to know the truth. Shakily I pulled back the bedclothes, at the same time swinging my legs rather carefully over the side of the bed. I stood up and much to my horror began to haemorrhage, the room decided to spin all of its own accord and blackness enveloped me.

How long I remained in this state I have no idea, except that when I regained consciousness the rest of the patients were being served afternoon tea. It was then that I realised I was desperate for a cup of tea. A nurse kindly obliged, and I think that if she had supplied me with the tea urn I could have managed to drink the lot. As I was enjoying my tea I glanced down the ward, and the sight which met my eyes made me freeze in horror and unbelief. My brain screamed, no not again! For there walking towards me was the same paediatrician who several months earlier had told me that there was nothing that could be done for Nicola. The situation appeared like an action replay. My mind reeled. If she told me that Melanie was dead as well, I wouldn't believe it. It couldn't be true, not again! God wouldn't let it happen, would he? He let it happen before, my confused mind told me. The doctor reached my bed, and sat down comfortingly by the side of me, tears rolled unashamedly down my face as I waited for the news that she had brought. Hesitantly she tried to comfort me as if she sensed the reason for the emotional state which her appearance had provoked within me, and quietly she told me that my new baby's life all depended if she survived the next twenty fours.

So she wasn't dead. I could have kissed her, for although the news was grim, my old philosophy of "while there's life there's hope" gently lifted my flagging spirits. So, all was not lost or as bad as I had first thought.

A wheelchair arrived at my bedside complete with a grinning porter, who informed me, that our first stop was the Premature Baby Unit. Excitedly, I leapt out of bed only to be told off gently by a passing nurse that any more of that behaviour and privileges would be suspended. I was so happy that at last I was going to meet my new little girl. We headed for the lift; many thoughts entered my mind, as I wondered what she would look like and what journey we had in front of us.

All too quickly we were entering the unit, my heart skipped a beat. I wondered if she would look so tiny and helpless just as Nicola had been in those last hours. Consciously, I pushed all these negative thoughts to the back of my mind and tried hard to concentrate on the words of the Ward Sister. She told me not to be alarmed by the amount of equipment around Melanie, or the fact that her hair (also like Nicola's) had been shaved off to allow an intravenous infusion to be administered via a vein in her head. She also did her best to reassure me that it was quite normal for a premature baby not to have finger nails, eyelashes or any eye brows, and that she was covered with a fine down all over her body. After she was convinced that I appreciated all these factors she took me to a small cubicle that housed an incubator in which Melanie lay.

My first impression was one of amazement for she was so tiny, and looked as if I were to touch her that she would surely break. She wriggled about, quite oblivious to the fact that her entrance into the cold light of day had caught everyone, me included quite off guard.

Chapter 7

NORMALITY

Within several days I returned to the safe haven of home. The bungalow that we rented two weeks before Nicola's death seemed strangely small and empty after the spacious and busy wards of the hospital. The stark reality of what had happened returned to me with a bump as I walked through the front door. Pathetically, when I had given birth to Melanie I had a secret feeling deep down that Nicola would return with me, and instead of having a busy, chattering toddler around me I was again left with an empty house and a premature baby still in hospital fighting for survival. Emotion overcame me as I sank into a nearby armchair; I did not have the strength to cope with this again alone. The events of the last six months had taken their toll; I had reached a point where I felt I could easily have succumbed to ending my life. The inner struggles that I had fought at this particular time questioned my faith in God and also in humanity. What was life all about anyway? What was the purpose of the individual suffering we all experience?

All night I cried, feeling increasingly sorry for myself, not being able to see any way out of the depression in which I found myself. Perhaps it was a good thing, for as the sun rose on another day I felt that the past was behind me and the future held a new beginning. Nicola would always be a part of me even though her physical presence was no more. My other daughter Melanie needed me and now came the time to be strong for her. Normality had to be regained, I felt this was essential else all would be lost and I would drown in an uncontrollable sea of despair forever.

Once I had made this decision I was determined not to look back, I would not say this time was easy, but it became more positive than the last six months.

Every day we journeyed to the hospital to visit Melanie; it was a twenty mile round trip. I enjoyed being out of the house and found that each day our daughter had made another step forward. Perhaps she had gained an ounce, or took all her feed and proudly brought up all her wind with a loud burp. But it was another hurdle crossed, for now was a question of living each day at a time, appreciating each moment for what it was worth. Nicola's death had taught me not to take anything or anyone for granted again. Isn't it strange but we do take everything for granted until we are stopped in our tracks and made to realise that nothing is permanent within our lives, and it is by our constant trying to make it so, that causes so much unhappiness to us all. If it were possible to accept what a day brings, joys and sorrows alike, without trying to change things surely we would have more peaceful and stable lives.

August Bank holiday Monday arrived, it was a special day. The mere fact that it was my twenty fourth birthday did not have much significance though. This day, all being well, would be Melanie's homecoming, mum, dad and the rest of the family came over to spend the day with us, mum trying desperately to hide her curiosity, for only parents had been allowed to visit in the premature baby unit, because of the obvious risk of infection. So, up until now Melanie had not been viewed by her proud Nanny and Grandad.

I had strict instructions to telephone the Ward Sister after the Doctor's round to find out if Melanie was to be discharged that day. One of the deciding factors would be if Melanie's weight had reached the required target of five pounds, for no baby was discharged under that weight. I rang the hospital at exactly the time I was asked to ring, my heart beating faster as Sister answered the telephone. Unfortunately the doctor had been detained so there was a further "nail-biting" delay before I would know if I could have the only birthday present that I wanted this year. Apparently Melanie's weight sadly lacked half an ounce, so this might sway the doctor's decision Sister quickly added, as if she sensed the apprehension in my voice.

To pass the next few hours away until I was to contact the hospital again, we decided to visit Ffrith Beach, a local attraction. The minutes dragged like hours until it was at last time to find out whether or not my hopes would be fulfilled. Eventually, after what seemed like an eternity, the Sister came to the telephone to let me know that it would be alright to collect my baby within the next half an hour. Grabbing a bag full of baby clothes en route, we reached the hospital in record time, and surprisingly enough mum never moaned at dad for speeding, looking back that was very unusual. They deposited me outside the unit, mum still winding her handkerchief round and round her fingers, a sure sign of how anxious she was becoming.

THE MOULDING OF A LIFE

At last, Sister told me that I could dress my own baby. How wonderful, bearing in mind over these eight weeks I had hardly been allowed to touch her, let alone dress her. Armed with nappy, vest, sleep suit and all the rest of the paraphernalia I charged into the small cubicle where she lay. I dressed her swiftly, all fingers and thumbs. All her clothes seemed to swallow her, she was so tiny. At least six inches of sleep suit hung from the end of her feet, and she appeared to have completely turned her head around in her bonnet until all that was visible was the back of her neck. Quickly I bundled her into a shawl, determined to leave the ward before anyone could change their mind and make me leave her there. All these weeks of waiting had finally paid off, at last I had my baby in my arms and no one was going to stop me taking her home.

I thanked the staff of the unit, after all words were totally inadequate for what they had done, and with a few brief instructions from Sister, I carried my little daughter out into the warm summer sunshine for the very first time.

Mum was unable to contain herself any longer, and rushed over to have a peep, making all the appropriate baby noises, which only women seem to understand, and then we got into the back of the car all set for home. I clutched my baby tightly, hoping now that this was a new start. This feeling of motherhood being extremely short-lived, as Melanie was whisked out of my arms, so that mum, bless her, could have a closer look, and count her fingers and toes, and anything else that might be in short supply. I wonder if this is a trait peculiar to all grandparents.

We arrived home, and all too soon it was time for mum and dad, who incidentally didn't get a look in, to leave. It had been a lovely day, in fact one of the best that year, and after I had waved them off on their homeward journey, I rushed inside to be greeted by the unfamiliar cries of a ravenous baby, who was determined to catch up on those extra pounds she so desperately needed to gain.

From then on my days and nights became a merry go round of endless bottles, nappies and baths! I didn't have much time to think, perhaps that was a blessing. By the time that I sunk into bed at night I was completely exhausted, only to be wakened at two o'clock for more feeds.

Eventually, after about eight months, the time came when it was necessary for me to think about returning to some form of employment. My husband worked as a car sales man, alright financially, if he made many sales, but his basic rate of pay was very poor.

I scoured the local paper for vacancies, and lo and behold came up with a nursing post in a nearby nursing home, the only snag being that it consisted of permanent night duty. That idea did not really appeal to me as I am afraid that some people are born to be "night owls", but I unfortunately was not one of them. In fact if I did not get my full quota of sleep, it was not unknown for me to become slightly irritable, to say the least. Nevertheless, I applied and was summons forthwith for an interview. It was only then that panic set in when I realised that I would have to find a reliable child minder as quickly as I could, or I would even be devoid of my sleep in the daytime. Luckily a friend of mine gave me the address of a middle aged lady, of whom she spoke highly, so I decided to give her a ring if the interview looked promising.

I was pleasantly surprised as the first sight of the nursing home caught my eye, it lay at the end of a long winding driveway, a large old black and white building with an east and west wing. From its position on the side of the hillside, it nestled in beautiful gardens, ablaze with a multitude of colours, overlooking the sea below. It was a very impressive sight. I was greeted by Matron, who incidentally looked quite young, but her face looked pinched with strain and worry. I assumed that it was the pressure of work, but I later found out that her husband had recently died quite unexpectedly, and so she had been left to continue the running of the nursing home alone and also to bring up her daughter Nicola, who was fourteen and a bit of a handful.

Matron ushered me into the lounge, a large spacious room, in the centre of which a grand piano was proudly displayed. The floors were all highly polished, and large patio doors framed yet another scenic view of the sea below. In every nook and cranny were exhibited a variety of Capo de Monte ornaments, mentally I noted to keep well out of reach of them, in case of accident. I had already formed an opinion of Matron in my mind after seeing her surroundings. It is strange how we often judge people by their possessions and actions. But in this case I could not have been more wrong, because in the months to come Matron and I became really good friends, not as employer and employee, but colleagues united in one aim, and that was to bring comfort and dignity to the aged patients which we cared for. My rota consisted of working four nights, from eight at night till eight in the morning, and then I had four days off. The wages were four pounds a shift, which I might add was a good wage at that time. The home had sixteen residents, some more mentally alert than others, my job was to tend to their needs, and I was also expected to prepare vegetables for the following day, do the washing, ironing and serve breakfast before going off duty. I really needed to return to nursing so I was very pleased that I had been offered the position. The only thing that I needed to organise now was the child minder, and surprisingly, that also fell into place almost straight away. I interviewed Mrs Crisp and instantly liked her, she had that reassuring, motherly attitude which I quickly warmed to her and so did Melanie. The final arrangements were made; Mrs Crisp would look after Melanie, do my cleaning, shopping and ironing and wake me at two o'clock before she went home.

I began my first night duty feeling a little bit apprehensive, but soon settled down nicely into the general running of the home.

I was introduced to the residents who varied greatly in their mental and physical abilities. Some required considerable attention with toileting and feeding, whilst others needed a friend to talk to and a sympathetic ear. This place had become their home and many were totally dependent on the nursing staff.

One of the great characters was a ninety two year old man, affectionately called "Grandad Morris". He was a bit of a lad as I soon found out when I tried to settle him down for the night after giving him his evening medication. As I tucked him in bed I had a conscious fight to remove his left hand which he had place firmly on the back of my leg, and was gradually moving upwards, while a toothless smile spread innocently across his old wrinkled face. I soon put pay to that, and decided to wear trousers under my uniform. For all his faults his heart was in the right place though. One night as I came on duty I popped into his room to say "Hello" and he beckoned me to come closer to his bed. A little wary by now, I approached with caution only to be confronted by "Grandad Morris" clad in his blue and white pyjamas, diving swiftly under his bed. Regaining his composure, and once more assuming the upright position he proudly presented me with his sputum mug which he had retrieved with such speed. Sputum mugs are not my favourite things at the best of times, so imagine my horror when "Grandad Morris" told me how thin I was, and how he had managed to save this for me from tea time. I feebly smiled, trying to humour him a little, all the while to my dismay he fiddled with the lid, his arthritic hands not having much of a grip, until off came the top and he fished out a large piece of toilet roll from inside the murky mug. By now I had become a tiny bit squcamish, especially when he told me to eat it later when I was on my own and had a bit of peace and quiet. Then he unravelled the toilet paper, and there lurking inside lay something vaguely resembling a piece of squashed Victoria jam sandwich. He lay back on his pillows, as if the effort of recovering the sputum mug from underneath the bed had been a little bit too much for him, and searched my expression to see if I was pleased with his obvious sacrifice. Beaming my gratitude and trying not to think about what else lay hidden within the dreaded mug, I reassured him that I would eat it at my first break, during the night. I remember how he squeezed my hand and smiled, Matron had told me at the nightly report that he had not been very well during the day. I mentally resolved to keep a close eye on his blood pressure during the night, and then went to administer the ten o'clock drugs.

"Grandad Morris" had been an inhabitant of Terfyn Hall ever since it had been opened so he boasted that he was its oldest inhabitant. The home was a private concern, so obviously he was quite wealthy. At his age he had seen many of his friends and relatives die, now one of his few pastimes was collecting their obituaries from the local newspaper and storing them in his wallet.

During the night that followed the "sputum mug" episode I came face to face with the dreaded obituaries in a very unusual way. It must have been around two 'o'clock in the morning when I started out from the office armed with a flashlight, to check the patients in the east, and west wing. I pushed open the door to the room where Grandad Morris slept, and took his observations, his bed was wet so I changed it and then settled him down for the rest of the night.

As was usual practice, I dropped the bed clothes, and pyjamas into the washing machine, switched it on, and went into the office to write some notes. The office was quite cosy but the lack of curtains made it seem somewhat sparse, I lowered myself into the chair, glad to take the weight of my feet. Sleep had been impossible the previous day as Melanie was teething and even Mrs Crisp had been unable to pacify her, so now the strain was beginning to tell on me. With my pen poised in mid-air, I had that distinctive feeling that I was being watched, but managed to persuade myself that it was easy to let one's imagination run away with oneself at that time of night, and carried on writing my report. Out of the corner of my eye and in the shadows of the night something moved! Jumping to my feet, I stifled a scream as my sleepy brain registered the presence of a lined, weather beaten face with small beady eyes staring at me through the window. Then I screamed and he was gone, as quickly as he appeared, leaving me shaking and decidedly scared. Matron had warned me that an old tramp sometimes put in an untimely appearance in the small hours, but he was harmless, so I assumed that this visitation had been him, well I hoped it was! Still shaking I decided to make a cup of coffee while I calmed down, and reaching into the pantry for the sugar basin, I thought I heard some scratching noises, I listened, and there they were again. What now I asked myself? The noise seemed to be coming from the cornflakes, the packet wobbled on the edge of the shelf, all of its own accord. I felt another scream coming on. I couldn't stand it anymore, so I threw the packet to the ground. What a mess, cornflakes everywhere, and in the middle of it all, a field mouse mesmerised by all the commotion. Yet another scream echoed round the Hall, as I decided whether or not to climb onto the kitchen table, watched by the tiny mouse that seemed to be enjoying the chaos he had caused. Bravely I thought better of it; after all it was only a very small grey mouse, with an exceptionally long grey tail. My first instinct was to make a dash for it, lock the door and pray that it would disappear of its own accord, but sense prevailed, I think, for a while all these jumbled thoughts of sheer panic went through my mind, the little chap turned on his heel and without more ado, disappeared into a hole in the skirting board. Very relieved I reached for that long sought after coffee and carried on writing my report.

It was not to be a peaceful night as fate had more things in store for me that night, as I found out later when I emptied "Grandad Morris's" bedclothes and pyjamas from the washing machine. What had I done now? There in the middle of the wet washing lay a soggy leather wallet, his prize possession. I did not really need to look inside to confirm my fears, because with my luck that night only the worst could have happened. I was right, it had! Gingerly, I undid the wallet only to be confronted with a wad of saturated pound notes all in one congealed mass, and even worse the dreaded obituaries in an identical state, the print completely obliterated. This was the last straw, my heart sank, perhaps it was a nightmare, and I hadn't thought that things could get much worse, but evidently I had been wrong.

Picking up some nearby clothes pegs, I slowly and carefully peeled the notes apart and I pegged them to an indoor washing line, situated conveniently by the kitchen fire. Standing back to survey the scene I wondered what our local police constable would deduce from the evidence if he were to walk into the room at that moment, for it looked like counterfeiter's printing room.

I managed to muddle my way through the rest of the very long, arduous night keeping a guilty eye on "Grandad Morris" and also his damp and dishevelled belongings. By the time that daylight broke everything was more or less back to normal, and the dried out contents of "Grandad Morris's" wallet was the only evidence of a night of disasters.

After that days, or should I say nights, were peppered with laughter, but I also experienced my fair share of sadness. Sadness in as much as "Grandad Morris" passed away suddenly as a result of a severe heart attack. His death left quite a hole in my life, for I had come to admire this rather robust, if not eccentric character. Furthermore, his sudden passing left me feeling as if

I had been a contributory factor to his untimely demise, by destroying his beloved obituaries which had seemed to give him strange comfort linking him with his friends who had gone before.

Another night shift and sadness once more lurked in the shadows to greet me along with the early morning sunrise. The west wing housed several patients, including Emily and Sarah. Two ladies who were both suffering from senile dementia. They scored a joint age of somewhere in the region of one hundred and seventy two years. Although they shared a large bedroom overlooking the beach below, and were in close proximity to each other every day, and had been for several years, they never uttered a word to each other. Perhaps, they were sadly involved in their own small lonely worlds, neither wishing to break the silence of their individual cocoon, which they had woven around themselves. Each night I had been instructed to lock their bedroom door as they were prone to wander around the nursing home. This was done for their own safety, to avoid them injuring themselves by falling in the dark. This night was no exception, I tucked them in bed, wishing them a goodnight and returned to my never ending task of washing and ironing. Where it all came from I never knew, but it was there every night, basketfuls of it, waiting for me. The night came and went, it had been uneventful, and soon it was time to administer the drugs, attend to the patient's toileting, and get them all up ready for the day staff, who came on duty at eight o'clock. Climbing the stairs in the west wing I decided that I would go straight to bed when I got home, it was the last of my four nights and the tiredness had somehow managed to catch up with me by my last shift. Opening the door to Emily and

Sarah's room I suddenly became wide awake, listening carefully as I undid the door I distinctively heard Sarah muttering Emily's name. That was extremely unusual because in all the time I had been employed at Terfyn Hall the two ladies had totally denied each other's existence. Pushing the door open quickly, I was not prepared for the sight which met my eyes for Sarah was perched on the side of Emily's bed, gently stroking her forehead, Emily lay back on her pillows, her face youthful in appearance and a feeling of peace radiating from her. She had died within the last few moments, and somehow Sarah had known something was not quite right. How ironic I thought, all this time they had been together, and now, when it was too late Sarah was trying to communicate with her.

We, as human beings tend to be like that, putting off those words of love, thanks or reconciliation until it is too late, and then we have to live with ourselves afterwards while the words " if only" echo around and around our heads. Then the opportunity is gone and there is nothing we can do to rectify the situation, it is too late, just as it was for these two old ladies. On a happier note, it was the custom for the patients to sit in the lounge watching television, or following some hobby or another, until bed time. It was a time for socialising for those patients who were able to be fairly mobile. It was during one such time that we were greeted by very loud banging on the front door. Matron and the rest of the staff had already left for home, and I must admit I was a little apprehensive about opening the large oak front door, wondering what was going to meet me on the other side. Nevertheless, there was nothing else for it but to open it because the patients were becoming alarmed now. Nothing prepared me for the sight that met my eyes as the door swung back on its hinges, for there framed in the half-light stood a rather enormous horse. It hesitated for a brief moment and then charged straight passed me, swishing its tail with extraordinary vigour as it went. Completely frozen to the spot, I watched as he sped into the lounge, dashing passed the grand piano and completely on course for Matron's prize possessions, the Capo De Monte ornaments. What could I do? The patients stared open mouthed; in disbelief as I shot passed them at an alarming speed, hanging onto the horse's tail. He quickly exited Matron's lounge, leaving a trail of disaster behind him. How I managed to steer him towards the open front door, I will never know, but eventually with a little coaxing I manoeuvred him reluctantly back into his stable. The patients had frozen in time they still sat there dumbfounded, unable to grasp why a horse should be galloping around their home, and even more why their nurse was flying round screaming attached to its tail. But again all's well that ends well, and Matron's daughter had quite a telling off for not making sure that the horse was secure before she had turned in for the night, and the damage, thank goodness was not as bad as it first appeared. Times like this left me little time for brooding over Nicola's death, but in all of my waking moments she was with me in my thoughts. Sometimes I'd see toys or clothes in a shop window and think how nice they would go with her fair colouring, forgetting for that brief instance that she had died. The word "dead" when used in context with my little girl stuck in my throat leaving me unable to utter that word and her name in the same sentence.

As I walked along the promenade, pushing Melanie in her pram, my mind wandered back to the sunny days when I had pushed a giggling toddler covered in ice cream along the same route. Sometimes whilst on these walks with Melanie we would encounter the odd frustrated mum with an irate child who was determined to obtain their own way over some such toy or sweets. It was only when I experienced the parent retaliating by giving the child a sharp smack or some such punishment to regain their authority, that I became angry, possibly because I had gained an insight into how impermanent life really was, and how I now regretted many of the times that I chastised or corrected Nicola.

All these thoughts were real, but looking back very exaggerated in my mind. It was very early days yet, and returning to work and having another baby seemed to bring a sense of normality to our lives. It was in fact only scratching the surface of many years of acceptance that lay ahead. Even though there was apparent order in my life, underlying it all, there was a feeling of hollow emptiness, a feeling that part of me was missing and could never be replaced. Life would never be the same again.

THE MOULDING OF A LIFE

Fanny and Peter Proctor my grandparents,
on their Wedding Day January 1915

Joan and Ron Patten (my parents) on their
Wedding Day March 1946.

THE MOULDING OF A LIFE

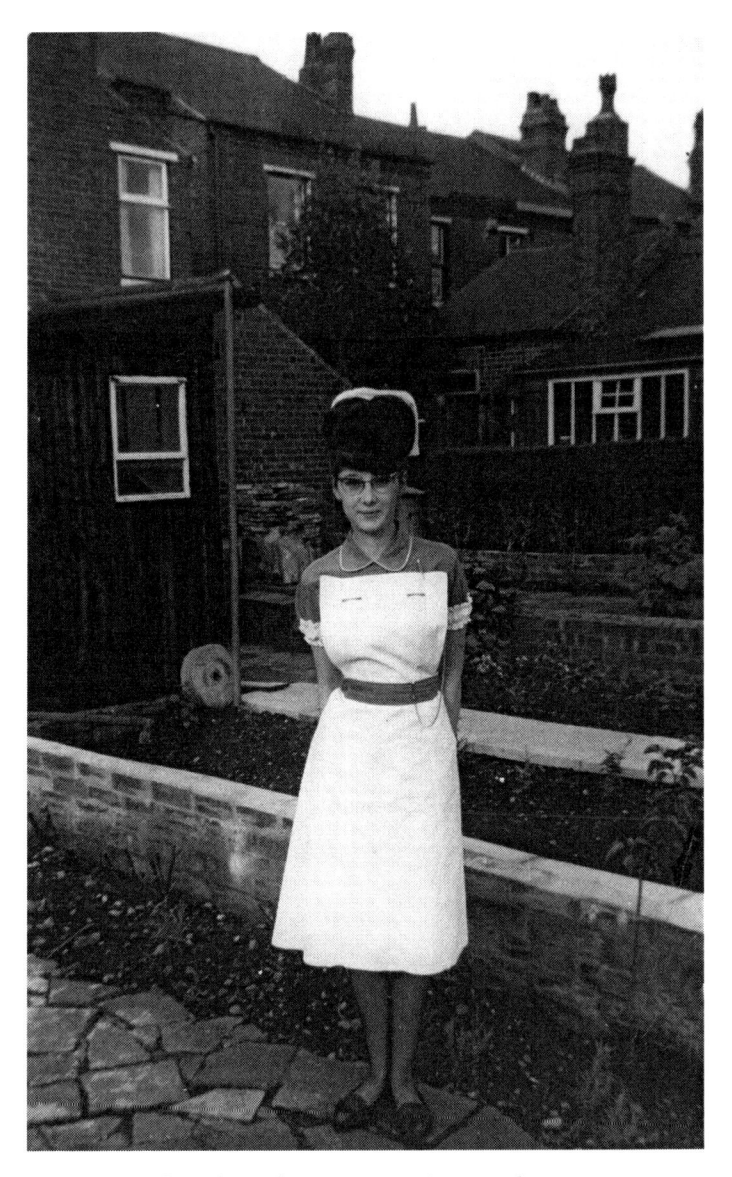

My first day as a nursing student.

My darling Nicola a few months before she died.

Four generations of the family at Jacob's fifth birthday party 2009   From left to right: my mum, me with Jacob, Mel, Chloe, Clare and Rhiannon.   Front row Kalum

Nancy and Jacob, two of my lovely grandchildren.

A proud day. My Graduation at Exeter University.

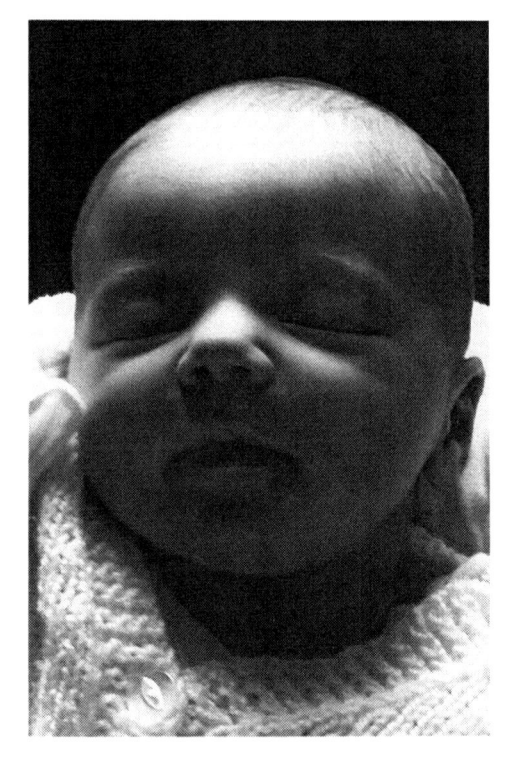

Our latest addition: Amazing Grace
two weeks old.

Chapter 8

THE ESCAPE ROUTE

Life plodded on in the same vein for several months, and even though I managed to fool other people and to a certain extent myself, things were not right by any stretch of the imagination. My marriage was floundering miserably; night duty was not being a great help either, as we became the proverbial "ships that passed in the night". I realised that my husband felt more at home in the company of the nurse with whom he had passed the long hours away, when Nicola lay dying. The strain of working nights and the long hours it brought with it, plus all the other factors served to make me increasingly depressed.

I began visiting the crematorium more regularly, perhaps twice or even three times a week, hoping that I might be able to glean the answers to so many questions which were still going round and round inside my head. Sometimes I felt as if it would burst, I can honestly say I really thought that I was going mad, this feeling pursued me and in retrospect, at that moment in time, I believe that I was on the verge of a nervous breakdown.

It is exceptionally easy during the early period of grieving to feel completely isolated in one's mourning, thinking that you are the only person to experience such feelings and also to feel that insanity is prevailing. It is perfectly normal to feel that way I later found out, and this bought some comfort along with it, because I realised I was not alone. Other people had been down this long dreary road too, and for many it still lay in front of them.

It also became increasingly difficult to live up to other people's expectations. They would imply that it was now time to pick up the pieces, with a new daughter, a new job and now this should be the beginning of a new life, completely switching off from the old one as if it had never existed. It was not that simple, even if I had wanted it to be, I had special memories of the two years I had spent with Nicola, and I was determined that nobody would ever take them away from me.

The crematorium was situated between Colwyn Bay and Conway, on a clearway which served for easy access from many surrounding towns and villages. It had only been erected recently, so during these early days much of the landscaping had not been completed. On dad's advice Nicola had been cremated. He thought that it was the wisest thing to do, in case we ever moved from the area, and with my track record, he was acting in my best interests. Her ashes had been sprinkled on the rose garden, so it was for this spot that I always headed, believing quite unmistakably I realise now, that I could be closer to her there. Each journey I made there, or should I say pilgrimage for that is what it had become, I resolved that I would be brave. Each time I left in tears, feeling that I had left her behind me, in that cold and empty place. Looking back all those years ago I realise that my daughter was not there at all. Why should she have been? She had never been there during her short life and the only connection I have with that place, is a cold, rainy, dull day at the beginning of February when her body was cremated. Having the knowledge that I now have, and as well as seeing Nicola twice after her death, I have not visited that place for many years, feeling able to remember her as she was in my own personal way.

But, at that particular time there was no other way out, but to run away from the problem. What I did not realise then was, that we cannot change anything by running away, for we cannot run away from ourselves, and eventually we realise that all we have done is to take all our problems along with us and probably gathered some more along the way.

We decided to return to Birmingham, and rented a small furnished flat in Edgbaston. It would do until we managed to get jobs and find something better. Bob was not impressed but I hoped that the move might bring us closer together by leaving his "lady friend" in North Wales, maybe now we had a chance to make our marriage work. After all I had married him "for better, for worse" possibly the "worst" was now behind us, and the "better" was due to come on the scene. How stupid can you be? Nothing changed, things were on a downward slope, escalating a lot quicker than I realised.

The flat was a far cry from the bungalow overlooking the Welsh hills which we had just vacated. It comprised of a sitting room with an unexciting view of a microscopic back yard in which there was a clothes prop and a small washing line. No sign of trees, flowers or any greenery. The kitchen was equally dismal and at the end of a long hall, there was one bedroom, in which we all had to sleep. It was fairly large in contrast with the rest of the flat, and the bay window overlooked a main bus route and a noisy junior school. The whole scene was dreary and so different in comparison with our previous home.

After several weeks my husband found employment in a local factory, the wages were not too bad so there was no real need for me to return to work straight away. This time I enjoyed spending time with Melanie who had grown up so quickly and was nearly a year old. But, alas gone were the walks by the beach and out into the countryside, now we had to adapt to the hustle and bustle of city life, which was so totally different. I remember going into Birmingham City Centre and being frightened to cross the road. It was quite alarming to see how conditioned we had become to the quiet, easy going ways of the country.

Eventually as Melanie became older, I returned to my nurse training at my old teaching hospital. This time though I began a part time course determined to complete my training so that I would have some qualifications when I finished it. This particular course for State Enrolment was geared towards married women, the part time hours an added incentive for nurses with a family. Sometimes I was required to work full shifts with more days off rather than work shorter hours each day and have just the normal two days off each week. Being back in the work I loved was great, but after about eight months it began to put a large strain upon our family life, especially when I was on duty over Christmas and Bank holidays. Sadly once again I had to give up the job I felt I was meant to do, but I knew that I had to put my family first. It was just as well I did, because one night just after I had checked Melanie was alright before I climbed into bed, I heard very strange choking noises. At first I could not grasp what was causing them, but when I turned on the light my blood went cold, as I stared in horror at my little girl in her nearby cot. She was lying there jerking and convulsing, her face contorted, blood trickling from the side of her mouth. She was wearing a pair of Nicola's pyjamas with Bugs Bunny all over the front of the jacket. It was like looking at an action replay of Nicola all over again. It took me several seconds, although it seemed that time had stood still, to regain my composure and take stock of the situation. It was too late to stop her biting her tongue as her jaws were already firmly clamped together, and the damage had been done. Showing my husband, who was just as horror struck by the situation, how to restrain her, I dashed out of the flat into the pouring rain to the nearest telephone box. My slippers became a hindrance so I lost them along the way, and reached the telephone box at the top of the road in record time. Imagine my dismay as I realised vandals had got there before me. The receiver hung from its cradle nothing but a mass of broken plastic, a tangled display of multi-coloured wires. It was at about this time I realised that the only garment of clothing that I was wearing my rather scanty nighty. Frantically I began banging on nearby doors in the hope that someone in the vicinity possessed a telephone. At that time it was only the more well off person who could boast of the luxury of owning such an object. Eventually a door was opened rather cautiously to reveal a middle aged lady also in a similar sort of apparel to that of my own. She regarded me from a distance asking the purpose of my business at that time of night. I hurriedly explained and her face softened instantly, as she stood to one side and pointed to the telephone on a nearby table. I wasted no time in calling the ambulance, and hastily thanked the kind woman and tore off down the street. My husband was still restraining Melanie, as she continued to convulse. It had really come as such a shock, so unexpected that the full impact of it had hardly had time to really dawn on us. I could see that even the strain was beginning to tell on Bob. His face was now ashen, and his hands were visibly shaking as he held on to our little girl.

After what seemed like a lifetime, the sound of sirens screeched through the cool night air and blue lights came to rest and dance on the bedroom curtains. The ambulance men were wonderful, they gave Melanie oxygen and we were off to the hospital in no time. We were both relieved to be in safe hands although a little bit apprehensive as to what had been the cause of the violent fits.

The Casualty Department one of the biggest teaching hospitals in Birmingham, and also my training hospital loomed in the distance, a welcoming sight. Melanie was quickly transferred inside into an awaiting cubicle, still receiving oxygen and still convulsing. The "on duty" Registrar had just arrived in the unit and we were ushered from Melanie's bedside by a kindly nurse, while he examined her. Meanwhile a hospital receptionist took a brief summary of her medical history from us.

After a short time the doctor emerged from behind the screen, issuing orders for various tests to be carried out, and medication to be given to her. Obviously I strained my ears but was unable to interpret much of his garbled message. They say a little knowledge is a dangerous thing, don't they? Within a few moments he came over to where we were sitting, perched uncomfortably on the edge of our seats. Both of us were expecting to hear the worst, that history was again repeating itself, each of us unable to voice our fears to each other.

The doctor seemed to be aware of our over anxious state, he had read Melanie's history and realised after the death of her sister we were extremely worried about our daughter's condition. He reassured us by saying that Melanie was convulsing because of a high temperature, known as febrile convulsions, which had started because she was teething. It had no association with the disease and circumstances in which Nicola had died. Nevertheless it was imperative that she be admitted for observation just as a precaution. We readily agreed, very relieved that it was not as serious as we had first thought. The next few days were spent in the Children's Ward, which had a strange atmosphere, combining a mixture of laughter mingled with sadness for some of its inmates and their parents. It was bright and airy, and very colourful, not in the least depressing as some of the adult wards.

Melanie's health improved rapidly, her temperature subsided and so did the fits. She was discharged on the understanding that it was vitally important for her to be given phenobarbitone until the age of five years, to prevent a reoccurrence. She never had another fit I am glad to say, and anyone who has experienced someone in that state I am sure would agree with me when I say that it is very distressing to watch.

We managed to resume some sort of normality once again within our lives, but Bob had started drinking quite excessively, and sometimes became violent towards me. I found this very hard to cope with, and one day when he returned home from work and said that he had found a better job, I thought that it might be the solution, knowing that he was not very keen on factory work.

However I had no idea what the other job could be, I must admit I felt quite excited especially when he told me that he had been offered a job as trainee manager of a newsagents shop on the main bus route into Birmingham City Centre. Here was a completely new start, and probably we could both work together in the running of the business. When he told me that we had to live on the premises I didn't think that was too bad, in fact I thought it would be great to get away from this claustrophobic flat. Maybe we had been a little hasty in taking it and moving away from Wales. As I look back I am aware that many people during a time of bereavement act in the same way, making sudden decisions in a confused effort to escape the sad situation in which they find themselves, and we had behaved no differently.

Mentally I was again making plans, when suddenly I felt as if I had been bought to earth with an almighty bump. What was he saying? The spacious flat above the shop was renowned for being haunted! He did not believe it he said, so I agreed with him. It was more than likely a story weaved by someone with a very over active imagination.

Still, as is usual in my life nothing is as simple or as straight forward as it should be, and I was about to find out just what life could be like sharing it with an unwanted guest.

Chapter 9

A SENSE OF EVIL

In the half light of the late wintery afternoon, the window display of the shop that we were about to view, looked almost inviting in the distance. Maybe I could describe it as a welcoming beacon after a disastrous start to our journey. Firstly the babysitter had been nearly half an hour late in arriving, and then when we were all set to begin our journey the car decided not to start, isn't it always the way when you are going somewhere important? In retrospect perhaps we were not meant to go, in a way I wish now that we had not! Today was very important to us both; we had passed the preliminary interviews with flying colours. All that remained was to visit the shop to see if we were happy with it and if the accommodation suited us. During our dealings with the Head Office of this chain of newsagents, both of us had been extremely impressed with the training we had received, and also the support we had been promised, should we agree to manage that particular branch. Uneasily I had a distinct feeling that we were being pressurised into taking that one shop. Apparently it had remained without a manager for quite a considerable period of time, coping under the watchful eye of an area manager, and also a relief manager who funnily enough, appeared to be in a tremendous hurry to rush off to "pastures new". Another office worker that we had met seemed very anxious to put us in the picture, "for our own good", he hastened to add, and seemed to relish in telling all the gory details. Apparently the firm had desperately tried to sell the property after a series of managers had left in quick succession complete with their families, each professing that the place was haunted. Needless to say the owners were not inundated with prospective buyers after this bit of information became public knowledge. Still it had not succeeded in daunting our prospects of a new job and home, so this was the reason for our visit, even if a little belated, on this cold frosty day in the middle of January.

As we passed the front of the shop, it appeared to be just another, ordinary newsagents. I do not know what I really had expected it to be like. I suppose that I had conjured up all manner of ideas from the things that we had heard although no one had actually told us in what way and by whom it was haunted, so perhaps our imagination had been left to do the rest. One thing we had both decided was that if we had the chance of a new start we were not going to let a supposed ghost stop us.

We toured the surrounding streets for quite some time before we eventually found a parking space. It was an extremely busy area being on a direct bus route into Birmingham City Centre. The road comprised of three lanes of traffic on either side of the central reservation, which we were to discover was always packed with heavy traffic from early morning and unfortunately, until last thing at night. Across the road from the newsagents stood a very select block of private flats, known as

Kennilworth Court, they looked very impressive and were surrounded by neatly kept landscaped gardens.

Either side of the shop were several other small businesses, one of which was a rather old fashioned ladies hairdressers, and the other an expensive ladies fashion shop. A public house stood on the end of the row, whilst just over the road I noticed a small branch of a major bank, which would be very handy for depositing takings in the night safe. I was aware of all these things as we walked with gathering speed towards the shop which was soon to become our new home. As we pushed open the door I was filled with an over whelming sense of relief, for it all appeared to be just a normal shop inside as well as out. There was nothing creepy or sinister about it all. The temporary manager rushed over to welcome us, ushering us hastily into the office which also served as a stock room. After a cup of tea and a quick chat we were ready to explore the accommodation. Ron, our new ally chattered nervously as he led the way up a twisting staircase covered in shabby threadbare carpet. At the top of the stairs he came to an abrupt halt, then regaining his composure pointed to his left and muttered something about being the bathroom. On the landing stood a well-used mop and galvanised bucket which he regarded with an apprehensive glance before proceeding down a narrow dismal passage. On the right hand side he pushed open a door to reveal a fair sized kitchen, this cast a little more light into the corridor in which we now stood. It did not help matters, or create a more cheery atmosphere though, as the walls of the corridor were painted in a dreary, dark green gloss paint, which looked as if it had been there since the beginning of time. Passing the kitchen we walked on only to see another flight of stairs which led upwards towards the bedrooms. At the end of the corridor Ron flung open another door which immediately flooded the depressing passage with bright sunshine. This was the living room; it was enormous, light and very welcoming. One of its features was a padded window seat in the big bay window and at the opposite end of the room a large ornamental fire place. Apart from these things the room stood completely empty, as it was to be let unfurnished. I noticed a door in an adjacent corner and leaving Bob and Ron talking, I opened it to find a spacious walk in cupboard. Instantly, as us women do, I began to plan what things I would put in there, when I suddenly glanced up to see written on the wall in front of me the words "You will be sorry" in thick, black marker pen. For a moment it took me by surprise, and then I decided that it was nothing but a childish prank, so I chose to ignore it and joined the others who were still busy talking business.

After several minutes we were invited to view the upper floor, and amidst its narrow winding corridors I located three large bedrooms. The passageway was dimly lit and after I had rounded a few corners ahead of the others I had the distinct impression that someone was watching me. I shrugged the feeling aside and opened a nearby door which led into the master bedroom, by this time Bob and Ron had caught up with me. Ron seemed eager to see what we thought about the attic. Personally I was mentally adding up how much cleaning there would be involved and was not too happy about the prospect of even another floor to cope with. Nevertheless I managed a reassuring smile as we rounded yet another corner to be confronted by a closed door directly in front of us. This was to be Melanie's bedroom there was a door to our left, half way along the corridor which provided access to the attic. The carpet was ragged and faded perhaps it had been a grey or green colour in days gone by, it was difficult to tell. A feeling entered my mind as if I had entered another era, somewhere I did not belong, and then suddenly without warning I began to feel very cold and shivery. The hairs on the back of my neck felt as if they were standing on end and I became decidedly uncomfortable, the urge to run away, to dash out of the building and put as much distance between it and myself overwhelmed me. Suddenly it was gone and everything seemed normal again. Ron gazed at me trying hard to attract my attention, I had a deep suspicion that he knew more than he was letting on, repeatedly it seemed as if he was scrutinising me to ascertain my reaction to different atmospheres which were present in this old building. I tried not to give my feelings away hoping that perhaps he might tell us what to expect if we decided to sign the tenancy, but he was so desperate to move on he was not going to jeopardise losing us as prospective managers in case he was left there indefinitely.

Casually he flung open the door to the attic to reveal a set of steep, uncarpeted steps directly in front of us. He gestured for me to climb them first and hesitantly followed as if by necessity more than desire. A blast of icy air hit me directly in the face as I mounted the first step. I decided that I would not be making any further journeys in this direction if we decided to live here. On reaching the top of the staircase I glanced around rather cautiously at first, not really sure of what would meet my eyes. In fact the only items of furniture there appeared to be in the attic were two old and dusty twin beds. Cobwebs were draped from every corner, the air was stale and damp, the whole place suggested neglect and emptiness, but most of all the poignant feeling which echoed around this room and vibrated from every corner, was one of loneliness, possibly sadness as well. The need to escape from the damp and suffocating effect of this room once more engulfed me. I muttered some feeble excuse and dashed down the stairs into the corridor below. Funny, I thought it had not appeared to affect anyone else, this strange atmosphere, but then I always had been a bit sensitive to things which might be described as paranormal, even though I was reluctant to admit it.

The others joined me commenting about how pale I had become, I laughed it off when my husband jokingly said perhaps I had seen a ghost. Once more in the comparative safety of the office, we sat around the table enjoying a welcome cup of tea which Ron had again hastily brewed. He was determined to keep us there for a little longer in order to win our confidence and persuade us to take this particular shop in order to release him from its pressures so that he could be free to take another managerial post somewhere a little less creepy.

Chapter 10

PSYCHIC PHENOMENA

A philosopher once said "There is nothing to fear, but fear itself". How true that saying was to become over the following weeks and months, because the more extraordinary things that happened, the more frightened we all became and things reached an unbearable pitch until we were verging upon a nervous breakdown and receiving tranquillisers from the Doctor. Anyway I am perhaps jumping the gun a little; I have not mentioned all that happened in between.

The takeover of the shop was a day filled with confusion, excitement and downright relief. With the weeks of packing and organising behind us, all that was left to attend to now was, unpacking and settling into our new, quite spacious home, at the same time the running of the business had to carry on uninterrupted. Glad to be out of the public eye I retired to the upstairs flat with Melanie to set about the mammoth task of sorting all our worldly goods. All the rooms such as the bathroom, kitchen and sitting room were situated on the first floor, connected by a windowless, winding, dimly lit corridor. A brighter bulb would sort that out, I muttered to myself as I dashed from place to place laden with linen or boxes of crockery. In the middle of all this chaos, Melanie played happily in the living room chuckling to herself and occasionally stroking our newly acquired member of the family, Baron, a German Shepherd Alsatian who would become invaluable by improving the security of the building.

Meanwhile Bob was signing all the necessary documents in the shop to enable him to take over as manager and Ron was also busy showing him various different order books. He seemed very relieved that his role of temporary manager had ceased and he could get away as soon as possible to another shop.

Donald, one of the paper boys appeared on the landing, he was of Jamaican origin although he sported a very strong Birmingham accent. He smiled broadly flashing a row of gleaming white teeth, shyly he wished us well in our new home and disappeared rapidly back down into the shop. Over the next few months Donald was to become more than just an employee, he became in fact a true friend and ally when we needed one most. The next couple of days were spent getting acclimatised to our new job and environment. It was all new and very different to anything either of us had attempted before. The regular customers soon got to know us and we began to feel at home. Head Office rang and suggested that I should attend a managerial course in a few weeks' time, so that I could also be proficient in the running of the shop in case my husband was ill or in need of a day off. It seemed like a good idea so I agreed. In the meantime I helped a little in the shop at the busiest times. I had to find a place for Melanie in a local nursery as soon as I could, because it was impossible trying to work in the shop while she continually played her own games with the chocolate and card displays. Luckily a nearby nursery said that they were able to help for a few hours a day, so I accepted readily and she began the next week. We were all becoming increasingly tired, what with the extra hours and lack of sleep. Melanie had taken to waking up every night at about nine o'clock and then refusing to go back to sleep. It had become a regular occurrence and I became more reluctant every evening to go up to her room to console her. I had this strange fear as I passed the door at the bottom of the attic stairs to reach my daughter's bedroom; there was an icy chill which stretched right into her room and all along the corridor. Wearily, one particular evening as Melanie's soft cries reached a crescendo of epic proportions I turned off the television and climbed the stairs aware of a black shape a little way in front of me, the hair on the back of my neck stood on end, Baron who was alongside me froze in his tracks, his fur bristling, baring his teeth in a protective gesture he turned on his heel and ran back downstairs. Terrific I thought, really given half a chance I would have been right behind him but Melanie's screams made me carry on towards her bedroom, the shape had now disappeared but an eerie chill remained. Frantically I scooped Melanie up into my arms and shot downstairs as fast as I could into the relative safety of the living room. Huddled in an armchair, still shaking, with Baron at my feet I tried in vain to pacify Melanie. Bob came up from the shop where he had been working on some orders to find out what all the noise was about; even he could not stop Melanie's screams. I do not know why I did it but I took my crucifix from around my neck and placed it on my daughter, her screams became more high pitched, until she was almost blue in the face, her little hands tore at the chain trying desperately to rip it off, I was determined to keep it in place and eventually after what seemed like an eternity, but was in fact only minutes, her cries diminished to a whisper and she fell asleep in my arms.

This happened every single night until I had run out of excuses which I constantly fed myself to convince myself that there was nothing wrong in the flat. My husband was also becoming worried especially when things started to vanish and then reappear in the most unlikely places. One evening when we were cashing up after a busy day, the "Stanley" knife which we used to undo the string on the bales of newspaper had completely disappeared. We hunted everywhere for it and when we could not find it, we gave up, mopped the shop floor and went upstairs to the flat. Next morning at five o'clock when we came down to take the daily papers off the step; we could not believe our eyes for there, as bold as brass right in the middle of the floor was the knife.

But you know how things are, sometimes if things are scary it's only human to look for a logical explanation and try to convince yourself things are not what they seem, so this is what we did. Until one day when we really could not convince ourselves any longer. It was tea time when the phone rang and an irate voice told me that they were ringing from Kennilworth Court, the block of flats directly opposite to the shop. The voice went on to ask if I knew that there was an elderly lady hanging out of our sitting room window, I suppressed a giggle and assured her that she must be mistaken, but the voice was adamant that she was correct. So, saying that it was impossible but I would investigate I replaced the receiver and grabbing an unsuspecting Donald I shot up the stairs towards the flat. I could not believe my eyes for there in front of us on the staircase was the figure of an old lady dressed in a long grey skirt, high legged boots and a green cardigan, her peppered grey hair severely scraped back into a bun. I could see right through her as she slowly ascended the stairs, suddenly she disappeared while Donald and I stared a one another in disbelief and without further ado shot back downstairs into the shop, both white and decidedly shaky. We told the tale to Bob and goodness knows how many customers who were in the shop at the time.

Now I was quite sure I had not been imagining things because there had been two of us who had both witnessed the apparition or whatever you would like to call it. Bob realised that we were not fooling about and told me to hold the fort while he went to investigate; I was only too pleased to do just that. Wild horses would not drag me up those stairs again at that moment. Donald disappeared into the corner of the shop to relay all the gory details to his mates who incidentally were hanging onto his every word. All of a sudden a large crash echoed round the store room at the back of the shop, this was followed by running footsteps as my husband came dashing back in. His face was drained of any colour, he was shaking violently and he was soaking wet! Muttering incoherently something about a mop bucket I pushed him back into the store room to find out what had happened; at the same time I beckoned Donald to hold the fort for a few minutes. Bob fell back into a chair and began to tell me what had happened.

He had gone through the store room and had climbed about halfway up the stairs to the flat when a galvanised mop bucket which we kept on the landing, came over the bannister, ON IT'S OWN, and its contents were emptied all over him. Difficult to find a logical explanation for that you might say, pretty impossible I would agree! I was now petrified. All that night the flat looked like "Blackpool illuminations", every light possible was switched on. Melanie's nightly screaming session happened as usual and I insisted on having a body guard with me every time I moved from one room to another. The cold patch at the bottom of the attic stairs seemed exceptionally icy and I did not linger there, instead I put Melanie into bed with us, and there we all slept a fitful sleep, filled with dreams of shadows and shapes of nightmare proportions.

Work carried on as normal, even though I was continually looking over my shoulder. I had to attend the managerial course at Head Office which was about an hour away from the shop. Mid-morning a rather distraught secretary rushed into the boardroom and told me to ring home as soon as possible. In my wildest dreams nothing could have prepared me for what had happened, Bob told me that there had been a bomb planted in the shop and the whole of the main road into Birmingham had been closed by the Bomb Disposal Squad while they diffused it. Petrified I was given a lift and sure enough there was a huge Army presence outside the shop. I knew that Melanie was safe as I had taken her to nursery before I had left that morning. Trying to get near the shop, proved to be extremely difficult as everyone was prohibited from the area. So I had to make do with phoning my husband who told me that the bomb was safely diffused. It had been planted under the card display behind a section housing fizzy drinks bottles.

I was really beginning to hate this place that we had made our home.

Footsteps, icy patches of cold and Melanie's continuous nightly screaming sessions were taking their toll on all of us. Even Baron, our "security guard" did nothing but lie whimpering in the corner. I had given up trying to entice him upstairs anywhere near Melanie's bedroom or the door to the attic.

One early morning I was making a cup of tea in the kitchen, Bob was in the shop serving the first customers of the day when suddenly, there was a low growling noise right by my ear. Well, there was no one else there, not even the dog, so I threw the tea into the sink and screamed as loud as I could. I was so scared, I half ran, half fell down the stairs into the shop still screaming and shaking. All the customers were staring at me as if I had gone completely nuts. Eventually standing in the stock room I managed to explain to Bob what had happened. He rang the newspaper chain and they sent someone out to investigate. They assumed someone had broken in, but I knew that they would not find anyone as whatever had made that noise was definitely not of this world.

Another day I was in the bath when a hand touched me on the shoulder, it had the same effect as the growling, and again I was reduced to a blithering idiot.

In desperation we went to a local vicar who came out the same night with a group of clergy and they performed an exorcism in every room of the house. This included the cellar and also the dreaded attic. The whole atmosphere changed, it became calm and warmer. We were so relieved. Several days later the local newspaper found out about the strange happenings and came to interview us. As soon as it appeared in the paper we were besieged by ghostly wailings down the phone and numerous strange visitors, who wanted to experience the happenings first hand.

A week passed, the atmosphere in the property was fine, and then suddenly it all started again. A lady claiming to be a medium arrived one afternoon and told us that she felt she needed to visit the place where all the activity took place. We tried to get rid of her but she was adamant that she could stop all the paranormal activity. My husband took her up to the attic as a last attempt to stop it all happening. After about fifteen minutes there were loud crashes, bangs and voices upstairs. My husband appeared disorientated and there was blood dripping from a cut on his eyebrow. The medium explained how they had climbed the stairs into the attic and as they returned back down she came out of the door and then it had slammed leaving my husband still on the attic stairs. She tried frantically to open it but it would not budge. Unexpectedly it flew open and Bob was thrown against the opposite wall. The result was plain to see, there he stood with blood gushing from a wound on his face, and already he had the tell-tale signs of a black eye forming. Doing what I did best I grabbed the first aid kit, patched his face up the best I could, arranged cover for the shop, and took him to the hospital where he had several sutures and a tetanus jab.. We were all very shook up by what had happened, so much so that neither of us wanted to go back into the shop. Realistically we had no choice, the medium that had been responsible for the reoccurrence, or maybe not, had long since left. So here we were again, knowing that the poltergeist was still in our midst.

I think things had reached breaking point, we had been advised by the Clergy not to involve the Psychic Research team, but we could not ignore this anymore.

Both Bob and I were living on our nerves, and now the doctor had prescribed drugs to calm us down.

Eventually we had no choice other than to telephone the Psychic Research team, who arrived that evening, complete with a vast amount of equipment. They detected that there was a violent spiritual energy in the property, describing it as a poltergeist. After further research it was discovered that two sisters had lived in the house in the previous century. They had shared the attic bedroom and after a massive argument over one sister having a lover, the other sister jealously pushed her down the attic stairs where she died. This had been the cause of all the psychic disturbances.

Within weeks we left the shop, unemployed and virtually homeless. Anything was better than living in that hostile atmosphere. We managed to rent a flat which was quite cosy but the toll of the terrifying situation that we had encountered caused a further rift between my husband and myself. Really we had not recovered from the shock of losing Nicky and neither of us had been able to grieve properly. Finding out I was pregnant seemed to drive us further apart, until one day he went to the shop and never returned. He had left me for a teacher who had burnt her bra and owned a motorbike. It would have been laughable but my whole life had been full of incidents where people I had loved had left me. I went through the birth of my daughter Clare, alone secure in the knowledge that I was never going to need another man again. So divorce was the only answer and when Bob pleaded with me to have him back, I walked away from that chapter in my life. Endless times I had forgiven him, but now all trust was gone.

Chapter 11

THE BEGINNING OF CLAIRVOYANCE

Some years later, I forgot my vow of not bothering with men and I remarried and gave birth to another little girl, and although she was born in Birmingham, we gave her the Welsh name of Rhiannon. While Melanie and Clare had dark hair and brown eyes, Rhiannon was blonde and blue-eyed, just like Nicola. On her forehead were birth marks in exactly the same place where Nicola had had the burr holes all those years before. Coincidence you may say, but I do not believe in such things, to my understanding, everything has a reason. Nicola and Rhiannon had entirely different personalities, when they were small and yet part of me wonders about another belief I have and that is reincarnation. I had the great privilege of attending a meeting where His Holiness the Dalai Lama spoke on reincarnation and compassion. I have much respect for such a humble, peace-loving and spiritual man. His words filled me with inspiration and an understanding of how simple, yet complicated life and death can be. It is vital to have an open heart and mind in our own perception of immortality and reincarnation.

I look at the three girls that I have now and wonder what might have been if Nicola had lived, but I also realise that she did not need to tread this path on Earth for very long as her Spirit was highly evolved. To my understanding once the lessons we need to learn on Earth are completed, we return home to the Spirit World.

Melanie has a special link with the sister she never met, as I was pregnant with her at the time Nicola died. She always buys flowers every birthday and anniversary of her death. The fact that she was always called "Starlight" has never been forgotten either, Melanie named a star after Nicola. Needless to say we both cried when she gave me the framed certificate of the position of the star. Nicola will always be a part of our family, even though she is not physically present; her Spirit is always around us. This has been confirmed many times by different mediums who know nothing about us.

The years passed and with three children to care for, I was unable to look more deeply into the way death and the Spirit world affects each and every one of us. Little things such a hearing my name being called as I dropped off to sleep encouraged me to begin my search in earnest.

As I became more spiritually aware I began to leave my body, or as it is known astral travel. Of course I had no idea what was going on at first but I was not afraid. These out of body experiences began one night after I had fallen asleep, when suddenly I found myself floating upwards. Before long I had come to rest in the corner of the bedroom ceiling, and I was looking down on my own body asleep in the bed. I felt quite calm and happy it felt very natural. This happened several times, after which I returned to my sleeping form with a jolt. We often leave our physical bodies during sleep, still attached by a spiritual cord, which us allows us travel into the Spirit World and later return to our physical body. Because we are more relaxed while sleeping we are more susceptible in allowing this to happen.

Six years later living in a different part of the country, I "saw" Nicola again, just for a fleeting second, out of the corner of my eye, there she stood. Smiling at me and then she was gone! Was it wishful thinking? No she was there as plain as day. So that was how my quest began, searching for the truth. Was there life after death or because of our fear of death do we want something more?

My introduction to the Spirit World came about purely by accident. I was inspired to write words of philosophy in short phrases at first, then in much longer paragraphs. Some was poetry, some was in Latin, of which I knew none, and I had to write it in purple ink for some reason. Every day the writing continued, waking me up in the night, and, on the way to work, even while I was cooking, it was never ending, it wore me out. I had no choice it just came into my head and would not leave me in peace until I had written it down on paper. One of the first things that I wrote was:-

"You are my mediator; through you I can assist people on the Earth Plane into a better understanding of life eternal".

This gave me a great sense of responsibility, but I was not sure what to do with the messages from my guide. In desperation I went to a service at a local Spiritualist Church looking for some answers. Sitting near the back, (for a quick exit) I was surprised at the number of people present. After some hymns and a short piece

THE MOULDING OF A LIFE

of philosophy, the lady taking the service pointed at me and said in a bellowing voice, "Lay down the pen, little one". All eyes were on me and blushing I stuttered "How did you know?" She explained that her guide had told her the exact words to say and that I would be able to understand what she meant. Well I really did, I was amazed!

She said that if I was an open channel, Spirit would come to me to make sure that I shared the words that they were giving me with others, but I must have rest as well. It was important to only to receive messages on my terms. The medium told me that my guide was a monk who had been a scribe within his Order, that was the reason he was giving me all this philosophy to share with other people to help them through their physical lives.

I was really impressed and left the service in time for my evening shift as a nurse at the local hospital. I was so excited that I told some colleagues who thought that I was gullible and it was a load of rubbish. They could have their opinions but I knew that this writing was not something which I alone could write, the terminology and the Latin phrases were not in my vocabulary.

I resigned myself to the fact that the philosophy was really important and carried on writing. There were many books of verse, philosophy and advice. My guide told me that he was a Franciscan monk called Brother Luke, born in 1816 in Italy. How fantastic and unbelievable was this? I was being inspired to write by a person who had lived nearly two hundred years ago.

My friends were amazed by the volume of writing that I had been given and eventually the local paper was knocking on my door. The journalist was extremely sceptical as he interviewed me and took my photograph which was published on the front page of the local newspaper the following week. There was so much work I was determined to find a publisher so that I could reach people with the words that had been given to me, as repeatedly I was told by Spirit they were not just for me.

"To each and all will come a greater understanding of the life beyond. A peace and tranquility will descend to each and every one of you as knowledge is revealed unto you".

Life continued as normal except for the writing, until I was invited to sit in an "open" circle at the local Spiritualist Church. I had no idea what it was all about, but turned up on a Tuesday night with about a dozen other people who seemed to know the drill. Everyone sat in a circle the lights were turned off with just a candle lit in the middle of the room. This seemed a bit drastic, I thought and scary but I closed my eyes as I was told to and sat there in perfect silence. Well at first I wanted to laugh as it seemed so absurd, sitting in the dark with a lot of strangers. Suddenly some words came into my mind, and then I had a feeling of being lifted up, so feeling very frightened, I called out to the lady who was in charge. She managed to calm me, and I really felt such a fool. Then she smiled saying that she had seen a monk close to me and I had moved out of my body. That was it, I was shaking, and when I reached home I told my husband that I would never be returning there again.

Several weeks passed and I received a telephone call from an international medium that lived near

Birmingham. She had heard that I was trance potential, so she invited me to go and see her. Part of me was adamant that I was not going, but deep in my mind I knew that I had to go. The day of the appointment came and I was nearly a nervous wreck. I made my husband promise to stay with me in case she put me into trance. How stupid I was, little did I know that my Spirit Guides were coming along with me. I have since learnt over the years that our loved ones and guides are all around us. The only reason that we cannot see them is because they are on a faster vibration than us. Although there are times when the two worlds come closer and our energies blend and we are able to communicate.

We arrived at our destination and were greeted by a lovely lady who sat and talked with me. She gave me a cup of tea, followed by a reading, telling me that I was capable of trance work, but advised me never to sit in an "open "circle as it could be dangerous for me. Not really understanding the difference between "open" and "closed" circles, she explained that an "open" circle is made up of different people each time, while a "closed" circle consisted of the same sitters, whose vibrations blended together, making it more harmonious for Spirit contact.

Trance is a state of allowing Spirit to take over your mind and body. This makes it possible for Spirit to talk with other members of a circle, usually closed, giving philosophy and evidence of life beyond the death of the physical body. Sometimes this is a light trance, called "overshadowing", where the person is aware of Spirit speaking through them, or there is complete trance where the channel has no knowledge of what is going on at all. After this meeting and still a little shaken, we returned home, wondering what was in store for me. Meanwhile the writing continued:-

"I shall tell you the works and learning which were given to me during my time on the earth plane a long time ago."

One day, whilst talking to a friend I was aware of random words popping into my head. There was urgency with the words and they would not leave me until I had said them to her. It was a message from her uncle who had passed away about a year before. In my mind he showed me a Christmas tree, so I passed this on, feeling a little bit stupid and she casually told me that he had died at Christmas. That was the start of the clairvoyant messages, which were received as mental images some in symbolic form. At that time I felt overwhelmed with responsibility because it is so important to translate the symbols given, exactly as Spirit wishes it to be relayed. It got a lot easier as I attuned my mind and blended with the energies in the Spirit World.

One day I began writing with such speed that I could hardly hold the pen. The words that were inspired from Spirit have helped me such a lot over the years and were the poem featured earlier in Chapter 5

No one, only a parent who has lost a child can understand the pain that loss evokes in one's very soul. One of the desperate feelings at that time is one of being helpless to help your baby; you as the parent are the one who is expected to make all things better. Not being able to fulfil this role brings with it an acute sense of failure and despair.

When the clouds of despair are around you, know that I am with you, as your light and guide.

These words that came from my guide really reassured me and gave me encouragement as I began my spiritual development.

I trained as a Spiritual healer but really struggled to accept that by laying my hands on someone Spirit was able to heal them, whether it be in body or Spirit. As I had been a nurse treatments were impressed into my mind. So it was very difficult to think that I need do nothing to heal that person except let Spirit use me as a channel.

Time passed and I was invited to make the numbers up in a "closed "circle. I am a true believer in the fact that there is no such thing as coincidence and everything happens for a purpose. So here I was and several weeks passed as I sat patiently in circle waiting for Brother Luke to give me some sign that he was with me. Nothing happened until one evening as I sat as usual in circle I felt extremely tired, there was a buildup of energy and a whirling sensation in my stomach. I felt as if I was drifting and then I don't remember anymore. Suddenly, I opened my eyes and realised that everyone was looking at me, they began gently asking me if I was alright. I said that I was fine wondering what all the fuss was about. Apparently I had been in trance and Brother Luke had spoken through me, explaining that he had been aware of the struggle I had of forgetting myself and clearing my mind, so that he was able to speak with them. The group had taped the sitting and I could not believe that this Italian, male voice had spoken through me!

I am me, you are you within us all is an inner self which cannot be pacified without reasoning.

How can I speak with you if I do not have infinite life?

Circles became my life, four or sometimes five times a week I attended, and went into trance and after coming round, listened to the tape of my guide speaking to the circle and delivering his help and advice. Many times I was told to share this philosophy and it is only now, that I have the opportunity to do so.

It seems that our lives are mapped out for us although we may not realise it at the time as we deviate from our pathway. My Spirit guides have told me frequently that we all have free will, which we do to an extent. However, in saying that, I realise now that I took a wrong turning, although a necessary one, during my life when I became a student Minister.

Working with a Minister as a bereavement counselor, made me realise how lonely people become when they are elderly or bereaved. It is a hard path to tread when you lose someone you love, but when there is no one to share the grief with people become isolated in their sorrow. Life takes a cruel twist when the ability to communicate feelings with others is lost. So again I found something useful that I could do. The minister I worked with was very caring but had never experienced a close loss. He always tried to crack jokes and believed that people should battle on, and after the funeral all would be normal again. I could see deeper than this because when the funeral was over and everyone returned to normality, the bereaved was alone with a limited amount of support, trying to get through the long empty days on their own. Even bereavement counseling can only do so much, but it gives that person a platform to share their grief and set goals for the future. I really wanted to be able to comfort them by communicating with their loved ones, but it was strictly forbidden to mention my own beliefs.

A year or so past and I was encouraged to go to study for a Theological degree. Training for the Ministry was quite a challenge, lots of studying with people so much younger than me, made me feel at a disadvantage. Preaching was involving me with the community, which was very important in my work, trying to put into practice the philosophies I had been given from Spirit. My sermons were not stuffy, with hard to grasp theology, I tried to bring everyday situations into the topics and I liked to think that the congregation could associate with what I was saying. The philosophies I used were Christian values interwoven with words from Spirit and were received very well, in fact so well that I was continually invited back to preach again.

One day I realised that I was being hypocritical; I was involved with the Church but could not accept all of its teachings. My mind made up, I left feeling very sad but I knew that this was not the right pathway for me. I started taking meetings in the Spiritualist Church, at first it was very nerve wracking, mainly because there was no preparation. In the conventional Church there was an Order of Service, with a prepared sermon. In a Spiritualist Church there was complete trust in Spirit to inspire philosophy and give clairvoyant messages. Most times everything was fine, except one night when I was taken out for a meal with friends. As we approached a building I saw a poster advertising an "Evening of Clairvoyance" with an "International Welsh Medium", underneath it had my name written on it. I was absolutely horrified and desperately hoped that it was all a big mistake. But no, Spirit had different ideas, although it had been arranged by my friends to help me develop my gift. I entered the hall and the great Welsh Hymn "Guide

Me Oh Thou Great Redeemer" was being played in my honour. I stifled a smile wait till they heard my Midlands accent I thought. I glanced around and the hall was packed there were over a hundred people in the congregation, all waiting patiently for a message from their loved ones. I was so scared that I tripped up the rostrum, or was I pushed? I'm not sure. Suddenly the music stopped and all eyes were fixed expectantly on me. I began to clear my mind hoping that I would be given some words, nothing happened at first. Then I looked into the congregation and I was drawn to this man whom I was "told" had tried to commit suicide. As I began talking with him, the words just came into my mind. The Spirit of his wife, who was very determined to make contact with him, came through almost straight away. Apparently he had become so depressed over the loss of his wife he had tried to end his life, and had come there that night to see if there was anything in this "life after death lark"? It was so fulfilling to see the relief on his face when he had proof that there was survival after death, and his wife was still close to him. After that I relaxed and let Spirit work through me, the evening passed with many messages giving reassurance that there was a life after death. Why had I worried, all I had to do was trust Spirit? After that evening I was always nervous before a demonstration of clairvoyance, but as I progressed Spirit gave me the confidence to share their words and teachings in order to bring comfort and healing.

I was very interested in Egyptology, however most Universities did not teach that subject. Luckily Exeter University taught it up to Diploma level so I enrolled on the Distance Learning course. I had no idea what I was

THE MOULDING OF A LIFE

taking on, there was loads of work but after three years I completed my course and proudly received my Diploma. Another three years study would give me a Bachelor of Arts degree. At first I was reluctant to commit to more studying as my father was battling with cancer at the time, so my first instinct was to end my studies and be with him as much as I could. Luckily the University was very understanding, giving me a period of time away from my studies to care for dad. He thought that I was not brainy enough to graduate, so after his death I set out to prove him wrong. He would have been so proud when I eventually graduated at Exeter, it had taken six hard years studying part time but eventually I had achieved it.

Darwin's theory of evolution and its comparison with religion was very interesting, as was my dissertation on "Victorian Attitudes to Death". Part of my course had included medieval history so I took advantage of researching all I could about monastic life. At the back of my mind as ever, were the words of Brother Luke.

Help is at hand, we walk with you in the shadows and the sunshine of your life. So verily, I say unto you go and spread my words of truth and light.

After finishing my degree I decided to treat myself and two of my daughters to a holiday in Egypt. There was a purpose to this as I wanted to investigate the Egyptian attitudes to immortality first hand.

Chapter 12

TIME TRAVELLERS

It was the traveller's ultimate experience. A chance to a discover an Ancient civilisation and to go back in time to a place that was full of mystery and intrigue, a place that for centuries had held the key to life in this world and the life beyond. Egypt was our destination, a land so different from the green, lush valleys of Wales, which we called home. Here, rainfall rarely fell on the parched hillsides and was a luxury it was not a nuisance. Daily life revolved around one of the greatest rivers that had survived for centuries bringing a security of energy to the land, people and animals of this country trapped in a time warp. We set off from our home in a small market town in Mid Wales. It was early morning, as the car sped past the darkened fields dotted with sheep and cows, a far cry from our destination. The plane was due to leave Manchester airport at seven thirty in the morning just as the world was coming to life. We were so excited, myself and my two girls, Mel and Rhiannon. Mel had always had this fascination with Egypt and her enthusiasm had become infectious. The plane soon left England far behind and we were crossing Northern Africa, in no time. Glancing down below at the cloudless sky, it was easy to make out the barren waste of the desert and sand dunes stretching for miles. A haze of heat rose from the land and suddenly we were aware of the stark contrast between the East and West Bank of the River Nile flowing below us. On the East bank it was fertile, bursting with vegetation able to support life, whilst on the West Bank it was barren and dead. It was here that the bodies of the Pharaohs of ancient Egypt were entombed and prepared for their journey to the afterlife.

The doors of the plane opened to reveal brilliant sunshine, the heat hit us as we walked onto the tarmac at Luxor airport. Armed military police were swarming everywhere; Arabs played a game of tug of war as they fought to gain control of our luggage in order to make a few Egyptian pounds profit in the heat of the day. It was forty degrees centigrade, a little warmer than we were used to, to say the least. Once on our way to the hotel aboard the air conditioned coach, we were able to catch our first glimpse of Egypt from the ground. There was a variety of culture to see, but the first thing that I became aware of was the poverty of the people who were working the fields and the poor condition of their animals, such as the horses used to carry water or people to their various destinations. Our coach reached the town of Luxor on the East Bank. It was busy with the hustle of tourists eagerly viewing the ancient ruins in Luxor Temple, or out for a stroll along the Nile Corniche. Egyptians piled onto the ferry crossing the Nile on their homeward journey to villages on the West Bank. Meanwhile in the heat of the early evening the children hassled unsuspecting tourists out for a stroll, pulling at their clothes, begging for money, sweets or pens. If they could obtain a pen then they were able to go to school, but the only problem was that every tourist who took pity on these children were usually besieged by ten or more others waiting to prey on their kindness. Our coach deposited various members of our group at different hotels en route; suddenly it was our turn. We alighted on the main road to be confronted by tourist police guarding the entrance of the hotel where we were staying. It had been described as a three star hotel in the brochure, but the first sight of it was so disappointing. As we entered the foyer the air conditioning, or lack of it was very off putting, in fact the atmosphere was absolutely stifling. Our room was dark and dirty with no light, probably because there was no window. After complaining bitterly we were shown to a light and airy room complete with a balcony overlooking the Nile and the West Bank. We agreed to take it as there was no comparison with the previous room. The porter muttered something in Egyptian and left. We later found out that this room cost seventy pounds a week more than we had paid and so this had to be paid before we left or else we would be arrested by those scary tourist police which we had encountered earlier. The sun was setting as we gazed out over the West Bank; it was a magnificent sight. Apart from a docked cruise boat opposite the hotel, I could imagine the splendour of a bygone age filled with ancient rituals, beliefs in an after-life and a dedication to spiritual Gods who were worshipped and adored by people who were so devout, a million miles away from our modern world.

After a sleepless night filled with fitful sleep, due to the continual rattling of the ineffectual air conditioning, we woke early, eager to explore. After breakfast we decided to venture out of the hotel. The tour representative had recommended that we always agree on a price before embarking on any form of transport. It seemed easy enough, but as soon as we emerged from the hotel we were bombarded by offers of taxis, felucca (boat) rides and also hailed by passing horse drawn carriages called kaleshes. The horses appeared to be walking skeletons and the carriages decorated like large brightly coloured prams. We decided to take a chance and visit Luxor museum in one of those carriages. The driver and I agreed on a sum of twenty Egyptian pounds for this journey and with as much dignity as we could muster, we scrambled aboard. Although it was only nine in the morning the heat was over powering and we enjoyed the shade of the canopy over the carriage. The driver set off along the road towards the bazaar and spoke to us in broken English. We clung to each other as we were thrown all over the place on the bumpy side roads. The bazaar was colourful and filled with many different aromas. Young men grabbed at Rhiannon who was only thirteen, offering me ten thousand camels in exchange for her. I readily agreed laughing wondering how on earth I would manage to take one camel home with me let alone ten thousand. Little did I know how serious they were, they were not used to seeing girls with blonde hair, and many times during our stay we had to fight off men and boys in order that Rhiannon might have some peace.

The driver of the carriage went further away from the bazaar, promising to take us to a "big shop" which we would "like a lot". Would we? We passed rows upon rows of horse's heads on a table for sale as meat. The girls and I exchanged glances trying not to show our distaste or to be sick. We arrived at the "big shop".

I tried to stifle a giggle, it was like small newsagents but in fact it was a jewellery shop. Shepherded inside by the driver, I caught sight of him exchanging a few hurried words with the owner, and then he was gone. The dimly lit shop was dreary and there were no other customers at all. I began to worry as the doors were locked behind us. The owner and another man bombarded us with items of jewellery trying to persuade us to purchase them. The girls and I were really scared, I did not want to buy any of the things offered, but I thought I better buy one so that we could get out of there. I chose a horrible looking cross with a scarab attached to the top. A good luck charm they assured me. Great, I nodded willing them to open the door and let us out. As if reading my thoughts, the door opened and we were out in the dusty street again being led back to the kalesh, and its' crafty driver who received his share of the profit from our purchase. Bidding the shopkeeper a hasty farewell we were off again, goodness knows where. All I wanted was to be back with the girls in the safety of our hotel, dingy though it was, but amongst other English people. The poor horse trotted onward taking us further away from safety, suddenly the driver drew in the reins and we were outside the museum. Safe at last, we quickly alighted the "large pram" and attempted to scurry into the museum where there were lots of other tourists, but before we could do so, the driver caught my arm and curled his lip into a smile, exposing his black teeth at the same time. "Madam I'll be waiting for you" he hissed in my ear. Determined to escape from his clutches I grabbed the girls and we dived into the museum.

Forgetting our adventures, the sight of ancient statues and also all the remnants of an ancient civilisation made up for all that had gone on that morning. We were absolutely engrossed in the treasures of the museum when I suddenly realised we had no idea where our hotel was, let alone how to reach it. We left the cool of the museum and emerged out into the heat of the midday. The sun beat down on us there was no shade in sight. The palm trees were scattered along the road at intervals while the drains and sewers delivered a pungent aroma. We tried to get our bearings. Suddenly with a flurry of dust the "big pram" and its friendly driver appeared as if from nowhere "Madam, madam", he shrieked, "I take you back". There was no escape, and feeling a little scared as we had no idea where we were it was quite a relief to see someone who did. Again we got into the carriage, no sooner had we done so, and we were galloping down the Nile Corniche again. I began to relax that was a mistake, for almost immediately the driver began demanding forty pounds. I was not going to fall into that trap, so I confronted him and told him the agreed price was twenty pounds. That was another mistake, the horse was suddenly whipped and the driver began screeching obscenities and we were hurdled from one side of the carriage to the other. By this time I was terrified and so were the girls, grabbing my purse from my bag I hastily shoved forty pounds in the driver's outstretched palm and gave into blackmail for the first time in my life. Suddenly the horse returned to a gentle trot and all was well with the world. We were deposited safely back at the dingy hotel with the driver smiling sweetly and offering to collect us again for another trip the following day. Not likely, never again I muttered under my breath.

That evening found us all with a violent stomach upset, we fought each other for the sanctuary of the bathroom in a desperate attempt to preserve our dignity. Little did we know that this condition was going to stay with us for most of our holiday and beyond? I had come prepared for such an event and had bought the necessary medication with me. However, the bugs that had caused this sickness and diarrhoea were much stronger than the pharmacist at Boots had envisaged and the tablets were totally ineffective against it. After a sleepless night we staggered down to breakfast, bleary eyed. We looked at the food on offer and the flies surrounding it and beat a hasty retreat. That day we had planned to visit Karnak Temple on the East Bank, so despite feeling quite drained, and always keeping an eye out for the nearest toilet facilities in a hotel we set out to explore. This time we did it in style, no more carriage rides, we hailed a taxi. The taxi driver took off at speed and we reached our destination within a few minutes. Karnak Temple was a splendid sight even in its ruined state. It was here that the ancient Egyptians worshipped Ra, the Sun God and King of the Gods. Major festivals were all celebrated here in this scared place. The entrance was guarded by an avenue of rams, which originally joined the temples of Karnak to the one at Luxor.

Massive stone pillars one hundred and thirty four altogether each stretching twenty three metres high and with a circumference of thirty three feet each, formed the Great Hypostyle Hall. This was a very impressive sight, each pillar covered from the base to the top in hieroglyphics depicting the Pharaohs honouring the Gods with scenes of offerings and processions. Some of the scenes were still preserved in the colours, which they had originally been carved. A massive crowd of tourists pushed us along, all marvelling at the ancient sights.

Eventually we reached the sacred lake where the priests of the temple had bathed each morning before beginning their daily prayers and rituals. Nearby stood a large statue of a scarab, originally there had been four but only one now remained. These had been placed there to commemorate the coronation of Alexander as Pharaoh of Egypt and symbolised the continuous nature of the rising sun. The girls and I grabbed an unsuspecting tourist and had our photograph taken next to the large stone insect. On our journey through the temple we were amazed at the number and size of the statues of Pharaohs and especially that of Ramesses 2nd which seemed to dominate the skyline. We wandered about marvelling at all the sights before us when suddenly a policeman beckoned me to him. Whoops, I thought what have I done wrong now? As I walked towards him I realised that he was smiling, he led me behind a stone pillar, and reluctantly I followed him. He pointed to a large stone obelisk and then pointed to my camera. That was a relief, he only wanted to show me where to get a good photograph, gratefully he took the picture and I thanked him. To my amazement he held out his hand for money, taken aback I took a note from my bag and pushed it into his outstretched hand. Was there no end to this constant demand for money, even the police? Perhaps I was too naive, I had forgotten that this was a poor country and the people here thought that if someone had more than them it was their right to ask for money. I found this very daunting in our stay in Egypt, perhaps if we had not been alone and female, and therefore vulnerable, we would not have been such obvious prey to the Egyptian men.

With all this in mind, the sickness and harassment, we decided to leave Luxor for the safety of a Nile cruise.

It was arranged that we travel to Aswan under armed guard to meet the ship, so that we could have virtual safety with other travellers. Even this had its drawbacks. In the early morning sun, before the scorching heat of the day set in, we left Luxor in a minivan with an Egyptian driver and his colleague. For a short distance we were in a convoy of several buses and vans until suddenly our vehicle left the safety of the armed guards and headed for the isolation of the desert. As we travelled through little villages, seeing the way that the ordinary people lived and worked it was quite humbling to observe the deprivation and poverty all around, and yet here was a way of life which was so uncomplicated without the hustle and bustle of our modern life. No technology dictated the pace of life; in fact it was as if time had suddenly stood still. The people were friendly waving as they ambled along on their donkeys, or carrying pitchers of water on their heads that they had filled from the River Nile. It was hard not to admire them as they carried on amidst an unforgiving landscape, in the unrelenting heat of the sun. This land was a contradiction of terms, it was a land of great wealth in as much as the great artefacts which it contained, but it was cheapened by the inability to market and portray these historical finds to their fullest extent. It was an area where at any minute the ground may yield another one of its secrets or treasures, no one could tell.

We journeyed on until it was time to leave our companions and board our ship. The cabins were adequate and comfortable we unpacked and headed for the top deck. The view was fantastic as we travelled past the green fertile fields on either side of the Nile. This river gave life to all of the local civilisation, the people, cattle and crops. It also enabled the transportation of food and goods.

Early one morning, before the over powering temperature made our journey unbearable, we visited the Artisan's village known as Deir el-Medina. Situated in the Theban hills, near to The Valley of the Kings and the Valley of the Queens, the ruins of this fascinating place kept the secret of the way in which many talented workmen and their families had lived. These people were responsible for the excavating and painting of the New Kingdom Royal tombs.

The village was enclosed by a wall and the workers' homes were generally tiny. During their working week the tomb builders often stayed in a small camp built on a ridge above the Royal valley, only returning home for holidays or at the end of their working week, which was composed of ten days. They were known as the "Servants of the Place of Truth".

There is more known about these humble workmen who cut out the New Kingdom tombs than about the Pharaohs, for whom the tombs were built. Some of the inscriptions and documents which have been uncovered show that over a hundred people, including children, inhabited the village. Some foreign names were found and there was evidence that a great many of the people who lived there were literate. Proof of this was evident in humorous notes and inscriptions. The presence of at least sixteen temples indicated that religion was an important feature of their everyday lives. One of the workmen's tasks was to build their own tombs. We were privileged to be taken down into one or so we thought, until we were suddenly plunged into complete darkness as we reached the sarcophagus at the bottom of the tomb. Everyone started screaming in fear until the lights were restored and we all rushed out of the tomb as fast as we could. We later found out that this was a common trick played by the Egyptian guides on many of the tourists. Most of the guides were giggling as we reached the outer area of the tomb but we were glad to emerge into daylight again.

Our visit was over all too soon and we were taken back to the luxury of the cruise ship. It was like another world, so modern and materialistic so totally different from the world that the ancient Egyptians had inhabited all those years before. Their belief in the afterlife was so apparent that it showed in their way of living. The beautiful decorations and inscriptions in the Royal tombs were a living monument to their faith and belief in a world beyond death.

The entrance to the Valley of the Kings is guarded by two very impressive statues, known as the Colossi of Memnon. These gigantic statues stand about twenty metres high and were originally built as part of a monumental avenue which led to the Temple of Amenhotep 3rd. It was here that our coach decided to turn round at the same time as another tourist bus, nearly crashing into each other. We were all rather shook up but as the two drivers leapt from their cabs to exchange insurance numbers, or so we thought, we were not prepared for them to begin a vicious fight in such a sacred spot. However, difficulties were soon settled and we were on our way once more.

After a while we approached a funerary complex set in a parched valley, it was partly free standing and partly cut into the rocks behind it.

This was the mortuary temple of Queen Hatshepsut, the Eighteenth Dynasty female Pharaoh. Unusually her reign had spanned over twenty years, other Royal women had ruled as kings before, but only when there had been no male heirs to claim the throne. Their reigns had been short and generally not included in the list of Kings. This funerary complex was originally built for her father Tutmose 1st and was set in a back drop of rocks which were spread out in a fan shape, behind the monument. At first sight it was extremely impressive. The temple itself was laid out in three terraces, each approached by a ramp. The walls displayed beautiful paintings of the life and childhood of the Queen.

As we walked up the ramp to the first terrace in the sweltering early morning heat, Rhiannon was on the verge of passing out. Her face was ghostly white as she swayed slightly and grabbed hold of my arm. We had all developed some gastric infection, but she had been the worst. Vomiting black water was nothing that I had ever seen before in my nursing career and it was very frightening. Rhiannon was extremely dehydrated, so we made for some shade and a drink, deciding not to explore this beautiful place any further.

Later the coach took us to the Valley of the Kings we were really excited as the highlight of our trip was to see the tomb of Tutankhamen, which was sometimes closed to visitors. Luckily it was open, so as the coach drew to a halt, we all stepped down into this final resting place of the Egyptian Kings. As we walked towards the tomb of the most well-known Pharaoh of them all, we were approached en masse by the local traders, who can be quite persistent in selling their goods. Rhiannon did the worst thing possible she vomited violently all over one poor man's feet. Needless to say he was not impressed, the visit to Tutankhamen's tomb was definitely not on the cards for Rhiannon and me so Mel left us sitting on the coach while she set off to explore. When she returned she explained that the tomb of the boy Pharaoh was small and really cramped. It was hard to believe that it had housed not only the final burial place of the famous Pharaoh, but also the vast amount of treasures which had been placed there to accompany the King to the afterlife.

Soon it was time to return to Britain bringing back with us an entirely different view Egypt, one of wonder at the treasures of an ancient civilisation, but also one of modern day poverty, but still a belief in life after death. We also bought back the illness we had contracted while out there, and all had a trip to the local hospital to have various blood tests for amoebic dysentery. Thankfully we recovered but strangely the mysteries of Egypt made us want to return, so a few years later, Mel and I went on a cruise which docked at Alexandria and Port Said. It was from here that we boarded a coach to see Cairo and eventually the Pyramids of Giza.

The journey was scary, leaving the ship at six in the morning, in a convoy and under armed guard, an obvious target for terrorists. Our coach had large signs on the rear which stated "English", not very reassuring we thought, but we were well protected and even had a man in a black suit with a machine gun balancing at the front of the coach as it sped through the deserted countryside.

After about three hours we saw them, the Pyramids, that is. I cannot explain how overcome with emotion I was at that first sight of such magnificent monuments to the Pharaohs. We have all seen the Pyramids on the television or in photographs but nothing prepared us for the immense size of them in real life. We clambered

THE MOULDING OF A LIFE

out of the coach eager to capture it all on film, and were instantly bombarded with locals selling everything from postcards, papyrus bookmarks to camel rides. We only had a short time there before the coach whisked us away to have a close up view of the Pyramids and the Sphinx. Tourists swarmed everywhere local children demanded our attention selling their wares. The Sphinx was smaller than it appeared on photographs and well-worn by the ravages of time, war and the sands of the desert. People and tourist police milled around, appearing like ants in contrast with the size of the huge burial chambers.

Opposite the site stood a burger shop, totally out of keeping with the ethos of such a regal place, a touch of the modern world intermingled with the Ancient land of two thousand years before. As we left there we all agreed that we had needed much more time to explore, but again we were on our way, being taken for lunch in a five star hotel. As we sat eating our meal the Pyramids loomed on the horizon it really was surreal. The last part of our journey was a visit to the Cairo museum. Here we saw the treasures found in Tutankhamen's tomb, golden ornamental chairs, his death mask and so much more. It was unbelievable that the little tomb in the Valley of the Kings, which some say was prepared in haste for the Pharaohs' early demise, could have yielded such an array of treasures.

I can honestly say that I felt nearer to immortality in those sacred places such as the Valley of the Kings than anyway else I have ever visited. Again we visited the tombs of the Pharaohs we had set off once more in the early morning hoping to avoid the extreme heat of the land that housed the secrets of the Pharaohs who were half mortal and half divine. The first tomb we entered was that of Ramesses 6th. The descent into the tomb was very steep and beautifully decorated, in the burial hall lay his shattered sarcophagus. The vaulted ceiling was painted in midnight blue and gold depicting the Goddess Nut swallowing the night and giving birth to the day. Symbolism was a very important way of portraying the beliefs of the Ancient Egyptians. This was shown in the colourful tomb paintings and hieroglyphics. Most times it told a story of the earthly life of the Pharaoh, his battles and conquests, and on his death, his journey to the afterlife.

As we completed our second tour of Egypt, visiting numerous tombs, mummified crocodiles, cats and Pharaohs, the ever poignant message of this land always echoed a belief in an afterlife. I think that this visit was part of my own personal journey which was predestined to allow me to appreciate that it is not only in the twenty first century that we are seeking some answers, but this has been happening for thousands of years in different parts of the world. I have decided that it would take a life time to explore study and understand all that was connected with the Egyptian beliefs. However, it is obvious that they as a people were totally in agreement that there was another life, after the physical death of the body.

Chapter 13

IN SEARCH OF MONASTERIES

Inspired by the Spirit World, suddenly, I was eager to research and visit places of worship. They ranged from the very spiritual Island of Iona, near the Isle of Mull, to Strata Florida, Abbey Cwm Hir, and Strata Marcella, all in Great Britain.

But my first encounter with real live monks began at the Monastery in Pant Asaph, North Wales. They had an open day selling all sorts of handmade goodies and wine. There was a singing monk called father Francis whose ballads were very melodious, and he had made some tapes of his songs to raise money for the monastery. It was here that I met another monk, father Rudolph, who surprisingly, had no red nose, but had a motorbike and sported a white beard. He supplied me with the phone number of his cousin who bred my favourite dogs, Scottish Terriers. It was thanks to him that I found my faithful companion "Marmite" who kept me company for thirteen years. Actually visiting the monastery put me in contact with a very good friend of mine Kevin, who had also taken his vows there. By chance he left the Order, married a social worker and moved quite close to where I live now.

During my nurse training I realised that one thing that we were not taught was how to cope with a dying patient and a grieving family. We all utter words of comfort to try to help people through the most traumatic of situations, but it never seems to be enough. So I decided to train with Cruse, as a bereavement counsellor and passed with flying colours. It was very difficult not to become involved with the clients, especially as we were not allowed to discuss our own beliefs. Several times I felt that if I had been able to share my experiences of life after death it may have helped that person come to terms with their loss, but it was not allowed.

I worked once a month at a local hospice alongside a Reverend, counselling the bereaved. A children's respite hospice was much needed in our area so we both began fund raising to make it become a reality, and along with many other people the dream materialised. The minister that I worked with thought that I should enter the Ministry by firstly taking a Diploma in Theology. However, I was never quite convinced that this was my pathway in life, and missed my gifts that had been given to me from Spirit, especially when the clairvoyance gradually disappeared. As I followed my short, but nevertheless exacting calling into the Ministry I was introduced to a wonderful man. His name was father Barnabas, a Greek Orthodox monk who lived in a monastery about eight miles away from my home. We had many a meaningful conversation over tea in the monastery. Once he came to a Harvest Festival Service that I was taking near to where he lived and afterwards we lived it up on tea and sandwiches whilst discussing the finer points of my sermon. He never criticised me, rather guided me in a gentle way. It was during this time

I met the Abbot, in fact I almost sat on him. Settling into a comfy armchair in the monastery library holding onto a cup of tea, I was suddenly aware that father Barnabas was pointing behind me rather frantically murmuring something about the Abbot. Blushing I realised that I was just about to sit on the biggest cat I had ever seen. He lay relaxed behind me quite unaware that I had nearly flattened him. When father Barnabas went away for a time another Brother looked after the monastery for him. He was dressed in the black robes with a tall black hat of the Orthodox religion. We decided to invite him for tea one day, I picked him up in the car and giggled to myself, because when he turned to look at me his head moved, but his tall black hat remained facing forward, as it touched the roof of the car. We all felt really sorry for him, his black boots were tied with string, and he seemed to be absolutely starving, ravishing all the food we put in front of him, as if it would be taken away if he did not eat it quickly. We totally missed the point of dedicating ones' life to Christ; it was all about not bothering with material things. Even so we fed him well and packed him off with several chocolate bars.

When father Barnabas returned he gave him a telling off, because apart from our little party, he had appeared on television explaining how to paint icons using egg shell as a medium. Again he had trespassed into the material world although I am sure that there was no evil intent. However he was banished to another monastery way up in the hills of Mid Wales. We never saw him again.

Father Barnabas came to Kevin's home once a week to take an Orthodox service. The tiny back bedroom had been converted into a minute church complete with a screen bearing icons. His over enthusiastic way of swinging the incense burner in this confined space set us all off coughing and choking, but it was all taken in good part.

Sadly father Barnabas died one day whilst taking prayers, the way I know he would have wanted to pass over. I feel honoured to have met and worked with him.

One evening I was watching television when I saw a beautiful monastery in a place called Ravenna in Eastern Italy. The mosaics and architecture were absolutely fantastic. It was so well preserved considering that it had been constructed around the fifth century. It was called the Basilica of Sans Vitale, and contained early Christian and Byzantine religious buildings, housing vivid fifth and sixth century mosaics, which now are classed as a Unesco World Heritage site. Suddenly I knew that I had to travel there to see this wonderful place for myself.

I booked a cruise that took in Venice, Croatia and Ravenna. It was a great itinery, considering the week before we left it was twenty six degrees in Venice, Mel and I took all summer clothes with us. When the plane landed in the morning it was only eleven degrees and rather chilly. Our cruise was fine, lots of excursions until the day came when we were docking at Ravenna. We were really excited anticipating the Basilica which looked nothing from the outside. In fact it was octagonal in shape, consisting of plain brick. We joined the large queue that had formed outside the entrance so that we could pay to get inside. We only had thirty minutes before our coach left for the docks, so we were quite eager to have a good look round and take some photographs. We eventually entered the Basilica of Sans Vitale. The mosaics were in pristine condition as was the church, it was breath taking. The walls were very high, lavishly decorated in gold and brilliant coloured mosaics, depicting scenes from both the Old and New Testament. The colours looked radiant as if they had been recently assembled. It was a place of spiritual importance and of great beauty? We only had ten minutes in this magnificent place; I could have spent at least a week there. Outside the church, we found a large Benedictine cloister that consisted of a vast complex of buildings that had gradually grown up in the church grounds between the tenth and eighteenth century. The architecture was extremely impressive; this was a very special place of pilgrimage. I will go back there one day, to take my time and look at all the treasures at my leisure.

Nearer home, is the little black and white timber Church of St Mary at Trelystan, standing alone on a slight hill, in the middle of a field about three miles from Welshpool. It is the only ancient entirely timber framed church in Wales. It consists of one single structure; originally it was constructed from wattle and daub. I can see that I was not led to this fascinating, spiritual place purely by accident.

As it happened a friend and I had stopped in a lay-by near the top of Trelystan hill when we saw a black and white building. It lay down a dirt track but it could be accessed via a gate and a walk of about two hundred yards. It was a lovely sunny day so we walked towards the little Church, passing lots of fragrant bushes covered with butterflies. The atmosphere was one of serenity; it was almost as if we had gone back in time. We entered the Church expecting it to be gloomy after the sunshine outside but it was bright and airy. The window at the altar end depicted a scene in brilliant coloured glass casting a rainbow of light inside the building and onto grave stones sunken into the stone flagged floor. At the rear were a stone font and a single bell dating back to the 15th century with the bell ringer's rope suspended from it. In the vestry was a barrel organ which could play twenty hymns, this was thought to have been made around the 15th century.

We discovered that the actual Church was very old and listed in the Domesday Day book. It stated that the burial of Edelstan, a Royal Prince, was buried there in 1010. It was also thought that later the Cistercian monks of Strata Marcella used Trelystan in the 13th century. Here was the reason I was guided to this beautiful place, another connection with monks which I had not expected as we set out that day. The field which lay nearby was known as Monk's Field, obviously named after the Order when they had worshipped there.

Brother Luke, who made himself known to me over thirty years ago, has always led me on a pathway where I have had opportunities to experience the sort of life that he had lived whilst on the Earth.

You were alone but now you have accepted me. Let me help and guide you to the truth.

PHILOSOPHY FROM BROTHER LUKE

God bless you again, my dear friends. As I draw close to you this eventide, I am aware of the melodious tones, which ring forth from your sanctuary of light. As it were you sing the prayer of Saint Francis, it is very beautiful. Do you not agree? Let us look more deeply into those words and perceive their true meaning. For, to become a channel for the true and beauteous peace of our Creator, we have to become love as pure as the spring morning, do we not?

For true love pure and untainted is a precious gift. As you wander along this Earth Plane in your service to your God you must perfect this channelling of love to all peoples of your world, whatever creed, whatever colour, and whatever religious belief. Do you understand what I say to you my children? For, if you can become as pure love you will then be able to achieve the radiation of this love to all souls within your world.

We know this is a mammoth task for some people are very difficult to like, apart from love, but by refining your Spirit within so will you achieve the making of yourselves unto pure channels.

My children, it is more better to forgive than be forgiven. If you can find the spark of compassion within your soul for another you have achieved much. Much more than you can at this moment in time realise.

I am aware that my channel is used to complaining of the amount of writing which befalls her, but I also know that within she is glad to receive the words of Spirit as they have guided her through many storms and battles. As if you listen carefully they will guide each and every one of you.

For I say unto you the words and experience you each receive from Spirit will within a short passing of the time increase, and these words will be for all not just for you alone my children.

I say unto you as my footsteps echoed within the stone floors of the cloisters, where I walked, I too questioned my faith, questioned my vows, and doubted my God, as you all do. I know these things to be a truth, are they not? For when you receive these words in a short span of time I wish you to ask of yourselves these questions and answer with an honest and humble heart, for by doing so you will become aware of your own faults and failings, as I did in many years of silence of the word, which occurred within my life span.

Sift out each fault within yourself and set out to improve of it. For as you do, so your character and failings will improve for the better. Slowly at first, but in the fullness of time the improvement will be of greatness.

My children I wish to speak with you this eventide but I am aware of your disciplines and so give thought forms to my channel to relay unto you. Please ponder on these I bring to you, and know that I am forever near to each and every one of you. Go forth into the sunshine of your lives and reap the harvest which awaits you.

God bless you my children, I give of myself to you in humility and love.

These are words received in Circle; obviously Brother Luke is Italian so his grammar is as it was received

Chapter 14

BUTTERFLIES, PEACOCKS, AND BLACK CATS

Symbolism is a very large part of Spirit's way of communicating with us, as I found out in a peculiar way.

My father was diagnosed with terminal lung cancer at the age of seventy seven. It was a terrible blow, unbelievable, that someone so full of life had been given a prognosis of six months. My mum would not accept the fact that dad was so ill, and tried to bury her head in the sand, unable to come to terms with his illness.

Dad was semi-conscious for the few hours before he passed away and I had left his bedside to go to the hospital Chapel to pray, while my sister stayed close to him. He had kept muttering that "the admiral was coming" we had no idea what he meant as he had no connections with the sea, so it did not make much sense. In the small hours he left us and we were heartbroken, even with the knowledge of continual survival it is hard to lose the physical presence of someone you love.

We took mum home all in a state of shock and disbelief. The following day we sat in the garden and a Red Admiral butterfly landed on a window sill nearby.

No one took much notice until about ten of them landed near us. We all looked at one another remembering what dad had said.

That week my home was full of Red Admiral butterflies, they were in the kitchen, the lounge and even in the car. I walked by the river and a butterfly landed on my coat sleeve and was still there fifteen minutes later. I was so emotional because I recognised this as dad contacting us to let us know that he was still alongside us even in death. As a result butterflies have become extremely important to us.

Once again we were aware of the Red Admiral the day before my mum passed away. Since my father's death she had taken to wearing his pyjama jackets over her nighty each night, so that she that felt close to him. This jacket was drying on the line near to where she sat staring and smiling at someone that only she could see. We noticed that there was a Red Admiral butterfly nestling on the jacket as it gently blew backwards and forwards in the breeze. Just over twelve hours later she had passed to the World of Spirit. Deep in my heart I knew that my father had come to take her home, so that they could be together again.

Butterflies are very spiritual, as they symbolism profound changes of the soul. The butterfly undergoes a massive amount of transition during its existence, from egg to larva to chrysalis and emerges a beautiful creature. This symbol of transformation allows us to understand our human state. As our soul or consciousness leaves the physical body, which can be regarded as a worn out overcoat, it has served its purpose of housing the Spirit until such time as all necessary lessons have been learnt, and it returns home to the Spirit World. It is here that it will be met by loved ones who make sure it undergoes a period of rehabilitation after the trauma which caused its passing. After this time the soul will learn lessons by seeing the effects of its actions upon the people that it was involved with during the time it was on Earth. Some people believe that after death we are sent to heaven or hell. This is not so, both good and bad people pass into Spirit and they are shown love and understanding, in order that they may progress through different levels to attain perfection. It is not known how long this process will take as my guide tells me that there is no conception of time in the Spirit World.

"If a minute was an hour and an hour a perfect day, how important is a second as we travel on our way?"
"Time has no meaning, space is all there is"

As we go about our everyday lives the Spirit realms are all around us co-existing with us on the Earth plane. The only reason that we cannot see our loved ones is because Spirit moves on a much faster vibration than ourselves. Spiritual mediums are able to tune into this world by raising their own vibrations to bridge the gap between our earthly world and that of the Spirit World.

One evening, whilst sitting in circle I "saw" a peacock it was very unusual and something that I had not experienced before. Its plumage was vibrant and its wonderful tail feathers a complete myriad of colour, as it strutted about in my mind's eye. Later that evening, I researched the symbolic meaning of the peacock and was surprised to learn that it is an extremely spiritual creature. It is used in various ancient religions to portray renewal and eternal life. So imagine my surprise a week later when

I visited a country house and there sat two peacocks preening, one each side of the door. If that was not enough I visited Glastonbury a month or so later and chose some oracle cards. When I opened them the first card I picked out was a peacock. I do not believe in coincidences so this was very strange. It did not finish there. I attended a hospital appointment at a well-known Orthopaedic Hospital in Oswestry, as I parked the car in the car park; a peacock strode past the bonnet and settled in the shrubbery. Thinking I was seeing things I asked a car park attendant who casually told me "Oh, that was Percy, we can't get rid of him, and he's been here years".

So there we have it, loads of peacocks, not something you see very often or maybe we do!

Loving birds as I do, I must admit I am not a great cat lover. Even so I was in a hotel in Somerset having a drink with my friend when a shiny black cat ambled over to me, looking straight into my eyes. I instantly felt a connection with it. Then it took me completely by surprise by jumping onto my lap, and snuggling down to sleep.

Recently everywhere I have been a black cat has walked in front of me I hope that is lucky as everyone suggests, but there is a symbolic meaning for black cats as well. They are supposed to be guardians of the home, how true that is I really do not know, although the one that made itself comfy on my lap changed my opinion of cats forever.

Chapter 15

THE CIRCLE OF LIFE

Life is not as straight forward as it first seems. We come into this world perfectly innocent with no knowledge of Spirit, as any previous incarnations have been erased. We choose our parents so that they can teach us the lessons that we need to learn. Yet our lives are moulded to a certain degree by all the experiences we encounter in our life time. They dictate our fears and insecurities for future days.

I have led what I think of as a very varied life, no different from most people who have their ups and downs. Although everything in life happens for a positive reason it is not always easy to appreciate at the time. Since I became aware of the Spirit World I can definitely say that I feel more confident that once this life is over it is not the end. To my understanding and from my communication with my guides I believe that we live only a short time in the physical body but a whole existence in Spirit. When we shed our body it allows our Spirit to be free, just as the cocoon which splits to allow the future butterfly freedom. When we leave this life, there is no pain or fear, worries don't exist anymore. Loneliness is not an option because people whom we have loved in this life are there to meet us and help us develop further. Brother Luke explained to me that he was lonely when he had taken his vows, but all that changed when he passed over.

My life was very drab and full of solitude. Often I questioned my vows, although I continued with my Order. I knew that there was more to existence, even believing in a life beyond death. The World of Spirit is so much more than you could have imagined.

When we pass over we will be surrounded by love, we will continue to develop our learning and progress to Higher Realms. We are shown the effects of our actions, good and bad on all the people we have met in our lives. The karma we incur follows us to our next incarnation.

When I have been working in trance or "see" clairvoyantly it is apparent how vivid the colours are in the Spirit World. This was confirmed for me again by guides through my writing.

The paint box of the world beyond cannot be compared to anything upon your Earth Plane. The brilliance and radiance of colour that comes from within, is as colour that you have never beheld.

Even though we all have this transition to make we must remember that now life is for living. We are here to gain as many experiences as possible and by accepting that death is a part of life frees us from fear. I remember that every message I received from a medium in the early days of my development included "Take one day at a time". Hard to do but with practise it can happen. I'm still trying and struggling with that one! Forgetting of one's self is also difficult, but to put other people's needs first is so important, unconditional love is by far the hardest lesson to learn.

It doesn't matter whether you are rich or poor do what you love to do, because when you die you will need to know that you have accomplished what you came here for.

Your life is yours, tread the path you wish but remember it has been allotted to you by Spirit. Take heed of your elders they have trodden life's road for much time before you. Not necessarily in the correct manner but they are older and wiser. Reason it out for yourself.

I have been told by Brother Luke that he has been with me all through my life and will be with me for all eternity. My awareness of him has made me feel secure and reassured me that when I pass over he will be waiting for me.

I wish to say unto you that as I myself passed into the Realms of light I was greeted by my loved ones, as I have told you it will be so. As you experience the feelings of extreme peace and freedom of the soul, you will also be a little apprehensive of that which will take place. Know that when that time comes I will be there to take of your hand and lead you across the bridge which joins of the two worlds. I am that close to you child, and as we talk I am impressed to say to you, have no more to fear, we walk now as one, you and I.

As I meet clients in my work as a bereavement counsellor the pain of grief is so obvious, even with the knowledge that I have loss is still painful. But when someone dies they are still around us, they still exist but in a different place. Visiting graves help us to accept their passing, but they are not there. Funerals are there as a celebration of life and to benefit the bereaved. They also serve to provide closure and acceptance but the Spirit of your loved one is probably standing alongside you, trying to console you. The most important thing in life is love and it does not cease after death. The bonds of love are never broken.

PHILOSOPHY FROM SPIRIT

Dear ones, we would speak with you again within the harmony and upliftment which we bring to you. The arrows of negativity, which you find aimed towards you, are there to enable you to gain strength and conviction of your faith within this period, in which you dwell upon the Earth plane.

We would say unto you that strength is but an illusion, it is present if you make it so. If you appear to have weaknesses, they are there because you have not yet overcome them.

We would draw your attention to the needless suffering and destruction of life within your planet, for we are aware of how this urge for power and material wealth has accelerated over the decades of your earthly time.

Many of you cannot imagine how time is of no importance in the Spirit world. It is non-existent, for there is no necessity for time as upon your Earth Plane. Thoughts are relayed and your earthly words are not needed. We think and so we become, we need no arrangements as we think and we are there. Many times it is incomprehensible when a Spirit returns home after leaving the physical body that the humdrum ways of your life on earth are no more. Ours is a peaceful existence taken up with learning *and guiding our friends who remain upon the Earth Plane until we are united again in the realm from whence they came.*

You fear death! Why is this so? Before you left the World of Spirit you feared the enormity of the task before you upon the earth, but once indoctrinated with the material plane and dense vibration, you fear the source of your very life. As you pass into the higher realms of existence, that fear will be quelled and will become a feeling of joy and peace, as you again realise the purpose of your whole being. For it is our observation that life upon the Earth Plane brings forth many worries, cares and encumbrances. Although it is a time of intense learning, the majority of you find it a time to be unhappy and full of woe. Others wallow in material gains that they can achieve and worship them as graven idols. Some realise their true purpose and endeavour to strive for that balance within their very soul. Whereby, they are illumined by the light of true love and this love is radiated forward to all people's with which they commune. It is to those people whom we wish to speak, know that you are truly inspired and guided and know that we are amongst you, but on a higher vibration. In time as you become more attuned to that vibration you will indeed know that we will be no more invisible to you and proof of a solid nature will be given. Do not be besotted by earthly things but rejoice in things around you which are given freely with God's love and power. Rejoice at all the wonders that nature has laid at your door and be not afraid of the morrow, but know with surety of heart that no one can take away that inner peace which has begun to build within, as a wall of protection from outside influences.

It is with these words that we leave you, but dwell upon what has been relayed to you, for you are all Spirit and we are all as one, even though we are not physically present alongside you. We can communicate with you, which has been proved many times. So gain your strength and peace within and be as the wild rose, issue forth a perfume so delicate and give pleasure to all with whom you come into contact.

In the love of the father we bring you contentment, peace and love, and bless you for the work which you do in your father's name.

I leave you with these words from Spirit and hope that they will enrich your life as they have done mine.

Lightning Source UK Ltd.
Milton Keynes UK
UKOW041655270513

211322UK00001B/96/P

9 781781 486054